T0072374

AMY'S REAL LIFE

HER JOURNEY FROM CHARLOTTE, N.C. TO TOKYO AND BACK AGAIN

JENNIE McNEAL

BALBOA.PRESS

A DIVISION OF HAY HOUSE

Balboa Press books may be ordered through booksellers or by contacting:

Balboa Press
A Division of Hay House
1663 Liberty Drive
Bloomington, IN 47403
www.balboapress.com
844-682-1282

Scripture taken from the King James Version of the Bible.

Scripture taken from the New King James Version®. Copyright ©
1982 by Thomas Nelson. Used by permission. All rights reserved.

Print information available on the last page.

ISBN: 979-8-7652-2700-8 (sc)
ISBN: 979-8-7652-2701-5 (e)

Library of Congress Control Number: 2022906290

Balboa Press rev. date: 04/18/2022

Many daughters have done virtuously,
but thou excellest them all.

Proverbs 30:29 KJV

For God has said "Never will I leave
you: never will I forsake you."

Hebrews 13:5 NKJV
(Amy's favorite Bible verse)

A thousand shall fall at thy side, and
ten thousand at thy right hand:
but it (the pestilence) shall not come near thee.

Psalm 91:7 KJV
(The verse spoken over Amy by her friend Jennie Hopper
in Charlotte, North Carolina, in 2017, three years before
COVID-19 pandemic)

CONTENTS

ACKNOWLEDGMENTS

I wish to thank so many people who helped me complete this book.

To our beloved daughter and son-in-law, Amy and Dillon, who gave me the inspiration. To our son and his wife, Steven and Mallika, who helped with navigating the sites so I could save my information.

To my wonderful husband, Jay, who has infinite patience with all my questions and needs. And to his dear, departed brother, Louis, who helped me with my laptop storage and encouraged me.

And especially to all of Amy and Dillon's friends who welcomed them back with open arms. And to our friends and family who prayed for their safe return.

And in the words of the psalmist David, King of Israel and Judah, "If I take the wings of the morning and dwell in the uttermost parts of the sea. Even there your hand shall lead me, and your right hand shall hold me" (Psalm 139:9–10 NKJV)

God is with us, and He loves us wherever we are.

CHAPTER 1

Thoughts of Tokyo

Why does everything have to be so hard?

You'd think when you make life decisions that would be the final step. Wouldn't you?

Oh, no. I believe, "with God all things are possible," as the Bible says in Matthew 19:26 (NKJV). But God also says, "You have to trust me and I'll show you the way." Oh, trust? Uh-oh, that means more faith, believing before seeing it happen, and that is not just a simple path.

Sometime in early 2016, our daughter, Amy, and her husband, Dillon, began the process of applying for Dillon to be transferred by his company, Ernst and Young (EY), to an international assignment in Tokyo, Japan. Since Dillon had become a partner for EY several years earlier, he was eligible to apply. Amy talked with us about being interested in an international tour that might happen when Zach and Matthew, their sons (our grandsons), would be in middle school. An international tour usually lasts for three years, so it followed that their family could be back in the United States by the time Zach and Matthew were in high school.

In March 2016, Amy came to our home in Georgia for a visit. We planned a birthday celebration for Zach, who would be ten years old on March 15. His brother, Matthew, who would be eight in April, was sitting at the table with us. After dinner one evening, Amy told us they had applied for this overseas assignment. Zach and Matthew didn't say much. They just had a deer-in-the-headlights kind of look, like they were still processing the information. As a mother and grandmother, I felt my heart sink because I would miss them so much. But knowing my plans aren't God's plans, I immediately began praying about this move.

In August, Amy and Dillon found out the funding for the move was not approved. They were very disappointed and didn't understand. But in October, the reason became clear.

Here I should give a bit of backstory. Born in 1950, I was the first child of my parents, Louisa Belle and A. Joe Snider. My brother, Joel, was born in 1952. My mother had rheumatic fever as a child, and as a result, rheumatic heart disease claimed her young life in 1959, at the age of thirty-five. In 1961, my dad married Patricia Summerfield. A year later, my sister, Leigh Anne, was born.

My mother, also called Mama Pat by her grandchildren, struggled with cancer since 2012. In 2016, after a major surgery and several rounds of chemotherapy, she rapidly declined. Jay and I went to Florida in the fall and were with my parents since the middle of October, although they were in separate places. My dad had fallen and broken his hip a few months before, so he was in a rehab facility. My mother was at home with help from home-health daily. We spent each day traveling from rehab to visit my dad and then to my parents' house to check in with Mama Pat's nurse and help there. On Friday, her home health nurse called hospice. When the hospice nurse arrived at their house, she said they would send a nurse every twelve hours as needed. I was keeping my brother and sister, Amy, and our son, Steven, updated with the latest news of her condition.

Amy called us and said she was going to fly down to be with us on Sunday. Could we pick her up at the Tampa airport? "Of course!" We drove to Tampa, and it was so encouraging to see her.

She was with us on Tuesday morning, when my mother died.

Joel and his wife, Cherry, had driven from North Carolina and were also with us. Stanley, my sister Leigh Anne's husband, had flown in from Minneapolis. I was so relieved that we had all of them there.

Steven arrived within the hour from Nashville. Then Rachel and Jordan, Joel and Cherry's daughters, flew in from Pensacola and Atlanta a couple of days later.

Amy had to go back to Charlotte for a commitment, but she was able to come back for her grandmother's funeral on Friday. Leigh Anne came in on Thursday afternoon.

The day of Mama Pat's funeral was bright and sunny. The graveside service was held at the Sarasota National Cemetery since my dad was a navy veteran, and military spouses are allowed to be buried there. As we pulled up to get in the funeral procession, we saw a beautiful structure with glass on all sides. Even the roof was made of all-glass panels that looked like wings. The building is a memorial for all the soldiers and sailors and their wives who are buried there.

A veteran on a golf cart guided us to park in line. As we approached, I saw my cousin Meg from West Virginia and her husband, Jim. We hadn't expected them to be there, so it was a nice surprise. Many of my parents' friends from their neighborhood and church were there too.

Joel, a pastor for many years, gave a wonderful eulogy. And my husband, Jay, a longtime church musician, sang "How Great Thou Art." Friends from Emmanuel Baptist Church, where my parents were members, provided a delicious meal for all of us. My dad enjoyed the meal but was ready to go back to rehab soon after.

It was like a homecoming or family reunion, even though it was a sad occasion. And best of all, Amy was able to be with us.

God knows everything, and His timing is perfect and sure.

CHAPTER 2

A Change of Plans

By 2017, I thought a door had closed on the international plans, but once again I didn't know the whole story. In early March, Amy told us that new plans were in the works. A few weeks later, Dillon's new position in Japan had been approved by Ernst and Young. She said they might move to Tokyo by early July. Only three months! They would have to pack all their belongings and possibly sell the house they had lived in for ten years by then.

Not only that, their family would be moving to Japan for three years, and we would only get to see them once or twice a year. Since I was semiretired, working two days a week, this was a real shock. I had been thinking we could get to spend more time with Amy and her family, not less. I would have to change my thinking and my plans. "For I know the plans I have for you says the Lord" (Jeremiah 29:11). His plans, not ours.

And even more changes were about to happen.

About a week later, Steven asked us to meet him in Sewanee, Tennessee. He liked to do a long run of fifteen to twenty miles on the trail near the university. He had gone to summer music camp at Sewanee in 2004, which is about an hour and a half from our house and a beautiful place for us to get together. So we said we would meet him for lunch at Dave's Modern Tavern, a restaurant there.

We had a wonderful lunch together. And before we left, Steven said that he had something to tell us. "I'm planning to move to Bend, Oregon, for the summer, so that I can train in high altitude and cooler weather for the Ultra-Trail du Mont-Blanc in France."

Talk about a shock! Both of our children, our son-in-law, and our grandsons were moving thousands of miles away during the same summer. It was a lot to take in.

Bend, Oregon, is 2,400 miles from our home in Summerville, Georgia. Tokyo, Japan, is over 6,400 miles away, and across the Pacific Ocean. Jay said it seemed like 15,000 miles. I felt like it might as well have been a million miles. *Help me, Jesus, to understand. How to think and feel. Be merciful to us, and help us.*

Later, when we told people about their plans, so many would say, "What a great opportunity!" After a while, our grandson Zach said, "I don't want to hear 'great opportunity' anymore."

Yes, we agreed. It's going to be a struggle to understand and comprehend.

Zach and I said a prayer together when I picked him up from a friend's house that summer. I told him that we need to follow what Amy and Dillon think is right for their future, and that God hears his prayers, and he can pray for God to help him through this.

I feel that children's prayers go straight to God's ears because they're so innocent and trusting. We know that God will calm our fears and help us!

CHAPTER 3

Japan Is a Go

Once the approval for the Japan move came, things moved along rapidly. Amy began clearing out items they no longer needed or could give to their friends. In order to have less to move themselves, they would sending most of their furniture and belongings in a large metal shipping container. The movers allotted about 400 cubic feet per person. Since there were four people in their family, that was 1,600 cubic feet. Placing a five-bedroom house full of furniture into a shipping container was not possible, so Amy and Dillon gifted many people with some very beautiful furniture. All in those three months!

They also decided to put their home up for sale. Their Realtor, Lisa, came over and gave them some good suggestions about how to arrange their furniture and to improve their chances for a sale. One of her ideas was to have the entire interior of their house painted. Amy and Dillon chose a pearl-gray color for the interior walls and white for the trim. The painters were Mr. and Mrs. Song, a Vietnamese couple who were very sweet and thoughtful. When we saw the finished product, it was beautiful.

Amy told us they were supposed to go to Japan for a week in April to choose an apartment and look at schools for Zach and Matthew. She asked if Jay and I could come to Charlotte to keep the boys while they were in Japan. I was delighted to say yes.

At about 6 a.m. on Friday, April 21, 2017, Matthew's ninth birthday, Jay and I left Summerville, Georgia, and drove to Charlotte. We arrived just in time to meet Amy and then go to the bus stop on their street to see Zach and Matthew get off the bus from Stallings Elementary School.

Since it was Matthew's birthday, I had brought him a birthday cake and made him chocolate chip cookies. Amy had bought him some gift cards for video games, so Matthew started playing some games on his computer.

Amy, Zach, and I went to her friend Jenny's house to help with her daughter Grace's birthday party. Jay stayed home with Matthew. The party was good with lots of games and good food.

When Amy, Zach and I returned home, Matthew's friends from across the street, Abby and Kate, were there, playing games with Matthew. Dillon was home from work too. Then we had cake and sang "Happy Birthday" to Matthew.

On Saturday, Zach's soccer team had its first soccer game in a tournament at a park. All of us went to the tournament. The day was sunny and beautiful. On Sunday morning, April 23, Amy and Dillon had to be at the Charlotte airport by 6 a.m. for their flight. They got up early, and before they left, Amy knocked on our door. Jay and I got up, hugged her, and told her goodbye. Amy and Dillon were in Tokyo for the next week and called us on FaceTime every day.

On Sunday a cold front came through Charlotte. It was 50 degrees and raining. It was our responsibility to take Zach to his soccer tournament. So we loaded our car with camp chairs and rain jackets and took Zach and Matthew to the park. Zach had two games, and it was a steady downpour through the first game. By the time for the second game, Matthew said he was cold and wanted to go to the car and stay, so Jay took him to the car. I went with Zach to his field and sat next to Brad and Kristen. After the game, Zach was totally soaked. I put my arms around him and held the umbrella over us. When we got to our car, we turned the heat on so Zach could get warm. It was good to get back to their house and get dry and warm.

The following Friday, we took Zach and Matthew to school and said goodbye to them because we were leaving for Nashville. Steven was running in the Music City half-marathon on Saturday morning. Amy and Dillon were getting home on Sunday. So their friend Kristen would pick up Zach and Matthew from school along with her sons, Jake and Jack, on Friday and keep them until Sunday. So glad it all worked out. The whole week went really well.

We would go back to Charlotte three more times before our precious family left on

July 3, 2017, to live in Tokyo for three years. In May we got to see Zach's fifth-grade graduation from Stallings Elementary School. Zach was recognized for winning the school's spelling bee two years in a row. He did really great! He and Amy studied word lists for hours every day before the contests. After graduation, we went to a Chili's restaurant and had a nice lunch. Kristen, Jack, and Jake came with us.

In June, we went back to Charlotte to keep Zach and Matthew while Amy and Dillon went to New York City to meet Sylvia, their relocation coordinator. They were also able to visit Howie, Dillon's ninety-two-year-old grandfather who lived in Connecticut. They had a good visit.

When we returned to Charlotte the last week of June, Amy had cleared most everything from their house. The movers had already picked up the furniture that would be shipped to Japan. We helped clean out the kitchen and took the last few items they were giving away to the Salvation Army.

All of us stayed at Brad and Kristen's for the last few days. On Friday, there was a big pool party at their community pool. We had a great time!

The next morning, we hugged Zach, Matthew, Amy, and Dillon before we left for home. They would leave for Tokyo in a couple of days, so it was bittersweet. But we knew God would be with them. And they were coming back for the Christmas holidays!

CHAPTER 4

Konnichiwa: Hello, Tokyo

On July first, Amy, Dillon, Zach, and Matthew flew out of Charlotte, headed for Tokyo, Japan. Amy kept us posted on their trip. They stopped for one day in Los Angeles, California. They decided to go to Santa Monica Park, where there were amusement rides and fun things to do. But Zach said he felt kind of uncomfortable because there were lots of people just hanging out along the boardwalk.

Zach's sixth sense about danger would come in handy about a year later. He and a friend were in downtown Tokyo for a Halloween festival. Zach noticed two young men following them after they left a store. Zach told his friend to come with him, and they wove in and out of the edge of the crowd so they could get to Zach's parents at his apartment. Thank goodness they were able to lose the strangers and get home safely! God gave Zach a good ability to avoid a bad situation. Thank You, Jesus, for your love and protection!

Amy and her family's next flight was from LAX to Tokyo-Narita airport. Everything went well, and she messaged us when they landed in Tokyo. She said the boys were really hungry when they got there, even though they had two meals on board the plane. There was a Burger King in the Tokyo airport, and they all ordered food and eaten there before heading straight to their new apartment at La Tour Daikanyama. Their rental furniture was already in place. When they got to the apartment, they could go to their rooms and crash. I know that was a good night's sleep.

CHAPTER 5

Leaving Their Kitty with Us

"Matthew, Zach and their kitty in Charlotte, NC 2021"

After Amy cleaned out their house in Charlotte and before they moved on July 1, they realized they needed to bring their kitty, Chubbs, with them to Japan. Amy contacted Sylvia, the relocation coordinator for Ernst and

Young, and asked what they needed to do to move their cat to Japan. It is a complicated process!

First, Amy had to take Chubbs to the vet and get all her shots up to date. They had to mail—not fax or email—all Chubbs's records to Tokyo. Then the kitty has to be quarantined in the United States with no contact with other animals for six months. Then she could be shipped to Japan. Now, after the COVID-19 pandemic, we all understand the word "quarantine" in vivid reality. But three years before, it was a novel concept.

After Amy saw that Chubbs wouldn't be able to go to Japan until close to January 2018, she asked Jay and I if we could keep her at our house until then. Of course we said yes. We enjoyed our time with their cat so much that we told Amy we could keep her until they got home from Japan in a couple years. But the boys and Amy were very lonely and missed her so much that we sent her to Tokyo on a plane in January.

Let's back up to 2012, when the family first got their kitty. Amy had been a CPA since she earned her master's degree in accounting in 1999 and passed the dreaded CPA exam in South Carolina. In fact, she passed it so well that she received the second-highest score in the state! Amy worked for several top-five accounting firms in her career, and, in 2012, she was offered a new job with the Elliott Davis firm in Charlotte.

Almost from the beginning, she began to feel unwell. She had severe pain in her abdomen and could barely finish a day at work without doubling over in pain. Her regular physician scheduled many tests, but they were inconclusive. So he referred her to a specialist in Winston-Salem.

After several weeks, Amy was unable to work and lost her job. The specialist diagnosed her with interstitial cystitis (IC), an autoimmune condition. IC is incurable, but there is a medicine that helps a lot and stretching exercises that also help with the pain. Eliminating certain foods from one's diet can also help with pain control.

Almost immediately, Amy began eliminating any acidic foods, such as tomatoes, from her diet. She went so far as to go acid-free, sugar-free, dairy-free, and gluten-free. She said, "Anything but meat and salad, and nothing that really tastes good." No bread or cake.

This was when Dillon, Zach, and Matthew thought of a way to encourage Amy and help her feel better. They went to the local animal rescue and got her a new beautiful black kitty with green eyes. When they brought the kitty home, we were staying at their house to help with Zach and Matthew, who were then five and three, respectively. The kitty was only a few months old and so scared that she went behind the dryer in their laundry room and stayed there for an hour.

Of course, this kitty became an integral member of their family, and I truly believe she has healing powers. Case in point: When Chubbs was staying with us in Georgia, I went through our front yard to get our mail from the mailbox. There was a rock barely above the surface on the path I was walking, and I tripped and fell. I got up on my own and told Jay and Steven what happened when I got back inside. For the rest of that day, the kitty wouldn't leave my side. Whenever I sat down, she would jump up and sit next to me. She truly understands when someone is hurting. Chubbs is a very special kitty. Oh, yes, I understand why they had to have her with them in Japan!

Amy was eventually able to add dairy and some sugar back to her diet without any ill effects. She still does helpful exercises every day and sees her specialist when needed. But the kitty was not negotiable. She had to be with them in Japan.

CHAPTER 6

Earthquake

On Tuesday, August 1, 2017, Amy called us from Japan at 3:30 p.m. in the United States. It was 9:30 the next morning in Japan. She said that they had survived their first earthquake, which happened 4:00 a.m. their time. The earthquake registered 4.5 on the Richter scale. This is considered a "light" earthquake that can be felt by humans and may involve some property damage.

I asked, "Earthquake?" I wanted to make sure I heard correctly.

Amy said it shook their bed, but she went right back to sleep. Dillon stayed awake for a while and texted his friend Brad in North Carolina to tell him what happened. Zach didn't even wake up, but Matthew said he felt his bed shake.

When Amy woke up, her friend Kristen, Brad's wife, called and asked her if they were okay. Amy asked, "How did you know that we had an earthquake?"

Kristen told her, "Dillon texted Brad."

Amy laughed and said they were okay. Then she told

Kristen, "I hope my mom doesn't know, or she will be worried."

But she called me anyway.

I asked if earthquakes were a regular occurrence in Japan. Amy told me yes, but their apartment building was one of the safest in the city. Most people consider Tokyo architecture not very attractive because it's all concrete and glass, but the city is built to withstand the tremors of most earthquakes.

She went on to tell me about the preparations the boys' school had in place in the event of an earthquake. The school has a two-week store of food and water. Amy said she bought an electric bicycle so that she could ride around the city, but also so she could get to the boys' school in thirty minutes if she had to in case of emergency. The school was seventeen kilometers from their apartment.

Emergency rations, kids being kept at their school, Amy being separated from Zach and Matthew. All this new information in their first month in Japan!

I'm praying now that this is never going to happen. Dear Lord, please keep them safe and protect them!

CHAPTER 7

Transition, New School, and New Friends

Amy, Matthew and Zach near Red Kyoto Arches.

One day while Amy and I were talking, she told me that she had a lunch date with Suzy, a new friend from church. Amy said the boys would eat lunch at home and then play outside in the park near the restaurant while she and Suzy had lunch. Praying for all of them to be safe today.

The next morning, Jay and I said a prayer for their safety. Then I realized that because of the time difference between Georgia and Tokyo, the lunch date had already happened, and all was okay. God knows our pasts, our present, and our futures!

Amy and I also talked about Zach and Matthew starting school at the American School in Japan (ASIJ) in the next few weeks. We know that this Japan experience is going to mature them in many ways. Praying for their safety, blessings, and protection in all things.

Jay and I went to Panama City Beach, Florida, in August for a few days to celebrate our forty-fifth anniversary. When we got there on Wednesday, it was sunny and beautiful. We were able to see a perfect sunset that evening. That night a storm front came through with thunder and lightning. It began a period of two and a half days of mostly rain. We went to the beach every morning, though, and enjoyed a few hours before the storms came in.

On Saturday morning, August 5, 2017, Amy called to wish us a happy anniversary. She said that she had a very nice lunch with Suzy, and Zach and Matthew had fun at the park. Our prayers were answered.

We started back to Georgia later that morning and got home to a very excited Chubbs. I FaceTimed Amy, Zach, and Matthew and showed them their kitty. She twitched her eyebrows when they talked to her. She knows their voices. Such a smart kitty.

A couple weeks later, Amy, Dillon, Zach, and Matthew had a three-day weekend because, according to Amy, Monday was Mountain Day, a national holiday in Japan. They family decided to go to a new restaurant that served Italian food. Amy said they really enjoyed it. She had sea bass, and the boys had pasta. She told us that the pasta was homemade at the restaurant. The whole family enjoyed the meal and the nice people who served them at the restaurant. They took pictures and had a good time.

Three years later, when they returned to North Carolina, they were talking to their neighbor, Tricia, who lived in Japan with her parents when she was a young girl. Tricia said that thirty-five years after they left Japan her dad returned to Japan for a visit. Her dad's last name is Barkman. Even after all of that time, the waiter at a Japanese restaurant they had frequented remembered her father and said, "So nice to see you again, Barkman-san." Adding "san" to your last name or even your first name is a sign of respect. It was so awesome that he remembered her father and she told us this wonderful story! The Japanese people could teach us all about being polite and honoring others!

But storms were brewing in North Korea, across the Japan Sea. During the first few weeks of August, the leader of North Korea was threatening to send or test nuclear missiles near our American territory of Guam. I looked on our map of the world and saw that Japan is located between North Korea and Guam. Our church said prayers for this region of the world and our nation at the end of our Sunday morning service.

The next day, the North Korean news said the Korean

leader had decided to wait and not test the missiles. We know that prayer changes things! Prayers were answered, and that part of the world is now secure, for the moment. Thank You, Jesus, for answering our prayers!

During the third week of August, Amy called and told us about visiting the ASIJ with Zach and Matthew. They took a taxi from their apartment to the school. When they got to the school, a Japanese security guard was at the entrance gate. Amy smiled and told him they were there for orientation. He said, "Ah, orien-ta-tion," and smiled back. Amy, Zach, and Matthew went into the school building and were assigned to Maya, a high school student who took them on a tour of the campus and showed them the schoolrooms and a nice courtyard area. She told them that there are about sixteen hundred students in the elementary, middle, and high schools combined. Matthew would be in fourth grade in the elementary school, where there were five hundred students. Zach would be in sixth grade and at the middle school.

Amy and the boys were told that Matthew would need an iPad, and Zach would need a MacBook laptop to use for their schoolwork. EY, Dillon's firm, would reimburse them. They went to the local Apple store and purchased the iPad and MacBook. Everyone in the store clapped for them after they bought their computers. Then they left the store, and it started to rain. Zach said, "I don't want my laptop to get wet and messed up the first day." Amy signaled for a taxi. After she, Zach, and Matthew got inside, the rain poured.

On the way home, Zach said, "I think the Tokyo American School will be good, except I just wish my friends from North Carolina could be here." Dear Jesus, give Zach and Matthew many new friends at their new school.

CHAPTER 8

Japanese Lessons and First Days of School

Amy's family near bridge and cherry tree in Tokyo.

Near the end of August 2017, Amy told us that she and Dillon were taking Japanese lessons privately.

The tutor usually came to their apartment but sometimes went to Dillon's office and tutored him there. Amy said that Japanese was hard to learn, but she was starting to recognize Japanese words when she went to stores. Like a few days ago, she heard another customer say, "Ninth floor," in Japanese when they were giving a location. Amy was able to give directions to a taxi driver who didn't understand English by telling him to go "straight" and then "turn left" in Japanese. I'm really proud of her for learning to communicate so well in the first month they've been in Tokyo.

Here are some English words and their Japanese translations that she told me about:

English	Japanese
mini	watashino
name	namae
husband	auto
master	shugene (what Dillon wants to be called. Haha.)
hello/good afternoon	kinichewa
thank you very much	aurigato godinemas

Not too long after we talked with Amy, Jay and I were in a Cracker Barrel restaurant near Atlanta. There was a nice family finishing their meal at a table in a corner near us. When we walked past their table, the Oriental grandmother said, "Aurigato." I recognized it as, "Thank you," in Japanese because Amy told me about it. It looks like we're all learning through this experience.

Zach and Matthew also have instruction in Japanese at their school several days a week. Amy told me that the day before, on Friday, had been Matthew's first day of fourth grade. Matthew invited one of his friends to come home with him one day. His friend's name is Kanato. When Matthew went to his room for a minute, Kanato called his mother on his phone and was speaking Japanese. Matthew came out of his room and asked Kanato, "Do you speak Japanese?" to which Kanato replied, "I am Japanese."

Kanato is now training in London to be a Formula 1 race-car driver, which is his dream. He has been in training to achieve that dream since he was ten years old. He lives in a boarding school in London while his parents live in Japan. Hopefully Matthew will get to visit him someday in London.

Amy said Zach went to the middle school to take a preliminary math test to see whether he would like to take sixth-grade or seventh-grade math. She rode with them on the school bus and said the ride took about forty minutes. Each school bus is monitored by one or two high school students who are trained in CPR and the Heimlich maneuver for helping someone who is choking. When they were on their way home, one of the high school monitors held his phone to his forehead and said, "Let's play Heads-Up, the charade game." Amy said one of the categories of the game was '70s rock bands. One of the kids said, "The Beastie Boys." Amy said, "No, that was the '80s. The '70s would be like the Rolling Stones." Then she said to Zach, "I'm probably dating myself."

"Yes Mom, you are."

Matthew had a good time with his class on the first day. He told Amy that one of the boys asked him if he wanted to be friends. Matthew said yes, and they played together on the school playground at recess. When Amy asked Matthew what his friend's name was, he answered, "I don't know." He later found out that his name was Keita, and his mother was a teacher at the school. I'm so glad God answered prayers for Matthew.

After Zach took his math test, he said it was okay, but there were several math problems he hadn't seen before. So he'll probably like sixth-grade math better. His first day of middle school is Monday. God help Zach to make a really good friend for life with someone in his class!

That same evening, Dillon asked Amy if she and the boys wanted to meet him at the Tokyo American Club for dinner. The Tokyo American Club is similar to our local mall, where there are restaurants, movie theaters, a swimming pool, and a game area where Americans living in Japan—expats—can meet and enjoy family life together. While the family was eating, Amy recognized a family from the boys' school. She introduced herself to the parents and found out their names are Clark and Annetta. They have two children at the ASIJ, Erik and Hana, in first and third grades. It's great that Amy and Dillon are recognizing people from other places in Tokyo who are originally from the United States. Amy said that at least three other families in their apartment complex have children who also attend the school. God will supply them all with friends.

The next Tuesday, August 29, Amy posted pictures of Zach and Matthew's first day of school. There was a good picture of them standing next to Dillon in the foyer of their apartment. Zach is getting so tall; Matthew is growing too. Amy also took a photo of them with their new backpacks while waiting for the ASIJ bus, and one of them climbing the stairs to get on the bus. It's about a forty-minute commute, so they have time to chill before getting to school.

Later in the day, Amy called us on FaceTime and said that Zach had a really good day and met a new friend named Aska (pronounced Oscar without the R). It turns out that Aska has been at the school for a year already and had a group of friends (eight boys) who he hangs out with. This means Zach has a built-in group of new friends since Aska asked him to join his group. That's great! They all ate lunch together and played soccer on the playground too.

On Wednesday morning, Zach asked Amy to make his lunch to take to school so that he could eat faster and have more time left in his lunch hour to play soccer with his friends. There is also a store near the playground where they can buy snacks. Zach bought a brownie there to add to his lunch.

Matthew had a good day too. He has Japanese classes at school every day. He learned that the Japanese word for one is *ichi*. So the name of the Japanese restaurant in Rome, Georgia, means "number one" since it's *Ichi-ban*.

Zach has Japanese classes three days a week. He's taking a band class too. Not sure which instrument he will choose, but he'll find out soon. It turned out that he chose the clarinet, the same instrument Amy played all through high school and at the Prince Avenue Baptist Church, her church when she went to college at the University of Georgia.

Amy said the shipping container with their furniture from the United States had cleared customs and should arrive today. It's an exciting day for all of them! She sent a picture of the apartment being cleared of all the rental furniture before their own furniture arrives.

The next morning was Wednesday, and Amy called and asked if we wanted to see their apartment with their own furniture in it. Of course we did. Since we were on FaceTime, she gave us a virtual tour with her phone. We saw her living room with their leather couches and a rug. Then she went to Zach's room, where he was sitting near his computer desk. He has a nice twin bed, dresser, and nightstand. His desk chair is black with an orange headrest. Zach said, "Hi," and then, "I love you." I always treasure these moments and never take them for granted.

Then Amy went to Matthew's room. He was sitting at his desk, at his computer, with his headphones on. He turned around and smiled. Amy said that he lost a wiggly tooth at recess on the first day of school. He still looks so handsome.

Amy next showed us her kitchen with a cute, flowered top, table near the refrigerator and a calendar on the table. She had decorated the stove handle by placing a pretty white towel with red flowers on it that she had bought at Bed, Bath, and Beyond in Charlotte when she and I went there in June. She bought placemats at the same time, which are dark red with white flowers. She had placed those placemats on her dining table.

Amy moved back to their living room. I saw a beautiful, red oriental rug under her couches. I asked her where it came from, and she told me, "We had that rug under our dining room table in Charlotte. Now we're using it in our living room here." It looked really good and is so nice and cozy. God bless Amy as she decorates their new home!

CHAPTER 9

School 2017, Week 2: Not So Easy

Monday, September 4, was Zach's second week of sixth grade and Matthew's second week of fourth grade. Since things had gone really well the first week of school, I thought everything at school should be A-OK.

Not so.

Tuesday morning, I got an urgent text from Amy. She said that Zach was supposed to give a speech in front of his English class, but he got choked up when trying to speak and asked his teacher if he could go and get some water. When Zach came back to the classroom, he sat at his desk and said he wasn't able to give the speech yet. So his teacher said he would work with Zach at lunch, and Zach could give the speech on Thursday. Zach also thought he had missed soccer tryouts. When he got home that day, he told Amy he didn't want to go back to school.

Amy placing a call to Zach's teacher and tried to find out about soccer tryouts. The school told her Zach could try out for soccer on Wednesday, but Zach decided it didn't feel right.

So he's not going to try out for soccer yet. It's disappointing, but at least he's learned to make his own decisions.

Thursday turned out well at school. Zach's teacher had worked with him on his speech, and when it was time for him to walk to the front of his class, his classmates began clapping for him. He got through the speech because his teacher asked him questions, which Zach answered. Questions such as, "Where are you from in the US?" and. "What are your interests?" When Zach walked back to his seat, the kids clapped for him again. Zach texted Amy from the school bus on his way home and told her it had been a better day.

Thank You, Jesus, for answered prayers and a wonderful, understanding teacher and friendly kids at Zach's school. They made all the difference. How encouraging!

When Matthew got home from school that day, Amy asked him, "How was your day?"

Matthew replied, "My teacher is great. My classmates are great. The work isn't hard. In fact, it's easy! It was good." So no problems there.

O, Lord, we know that you have special plans for Zach's and Matthew's lives. Sometimes life is hard, and other times not. Help Zach to rise above his difficulties, and thank You for his friends. Thank You that they both have good teachers who want to help them. Praying for grace, mercy, and wisdom every day. Help us, Jesus!

Amy told us she had a busy week and went to the school twice for separate meetings with Zach's and Matthew's teachers about curriculum advisement. She also met a friend for lunch that day. Amy said her friend told her about a store in Tokyo where she could find clothes for Zach and

Matthew. Amy had told me that it was easy to find clothes for adults and babies but not so easy to find children and youth sizes. Her friend told Amy about a store called Next. Amy went there and bought four shirts each for Zach and Matthew. She was so excited!

At Matthew's curriculum meeting, Amy was told that his class needed one more room mother. Amy said that she could help with that. That will be fun for both her and Matthew!

Prayers are being answered for their new roles in Japan. Thank You, Jesus!

A Bible verse came to mind during this time.

> "The Lord is close to the brokenhearted;
> He rescues those whose spirits are crushed.
> Psalm 34:18 NIV

Amy told me that there were Kintsugi classes at the Tokyo American Club. Kintsugi or golden joinery is the Japanese art of repairing broken pottery by mending the area of breakage with lacquer dusted or mixed with powdered gold, silver or platinum. As a philosophy, it treats breakage and repair as a part of the history of an object, rather than something to disguise.

One theory is that Kintsugi may have originated when a Japanese shogun Ashikaga Yoshimasa sent a damaged Chinese tea bowl back to China for repairs in the late 15th century. When it was returned, repaired with ugly metal staples, it may have prompted Japanese craftsmen to look for a more aesthetically pleasing means of repair.

Kintsugi makes the broken object more beautiful.

> Psalm 147:3 NIV says "He heals the brokenhearted and binds up their wounds."

CHAPTER 10

Our Second Trip Out West and an Unexpected Call

On September 17, 2017, Jay and I went to church and had a good Sunday school lesson on Noah and the ark. In the church worship service, our choir sang, "God Said You're Going to Make It." I really needed to hear that since we were going to travel all the way across the United States to Oregon and back in the next two weeks.

Our son, Steven, is an ultrarunner and would be competing in his third 100-mile race near Olallie Lake, Oregon. We were going there to be his support "crew "and help hand him supplies and food at various points along the race route. I arranged for a hotel room in every city we would be near each evening on our trip. Except Denver, Colorado, where my sister, Leigh Anne, lived with her husband, Stanley. We would stay at their condo. We would stay with Steven at his condo in Bend, Oregon, when we arrived there.

Everything went well on our trip. Steven had his best 100-mile race with a good finish time of thirty-one hours.

Of 152 runners who began the race, there were 81 finishers and 71 who did not finish (DNF). This was probably due to an unexpected snowfall of six inches the night before the race started, which made the course more treacherous. It was a good thing Steven had trekking poles (like ski poles) that helped him navigate the trails. We're so happy for him that he finished well. This was a qualifying race to enable him to register for his "dream" 100-mile race in France called the UTMB-Ultra trail du Mont Blanc.

Author's note: My first book, *Steven: A Runner's Life,* explains his journey as an ultrarunner and our trip to France in 2018.

After the race, Jay and I stayed at Steven's condo for a few days while Steven recovered from the race. We went to several fun places in Bend, like the Old Mill district and the Flag bridge over the beautiful Deschutes River near downtown.

On Wednesday, September 27, 2017, we packed our luggage in our cars for our trip to Sacramento, California. We left for California around 9:00 a.m., with Steven leading the way on US 97 in his Pathfinder. We followed in our car all the way through Oregon to California. The drive was beautiful. We saw signs to Crater Lake National Park. Though we didn't stop there, we could see beautiful views. The temperature had been 43 degrees when we left the Bend area, but it was 85 degrees when we stopped for lunch in northern California. It felt amazing to stand outside and enjoy the sunshine and feel the breeze, I know why people want to live there!

We continued to Sacramento through heavy rush-hour traffic. We ate dinner at Famous Burger, and then Steven went to meet a friend, Michael, who he had met in Nashville but now lived in Sacramento. When Steven came back to our room, he said Michael suggested we should also visit Napa Valley since we were going to San Francisco the next day. He said, "You have to stop and see Napa. It's within ten miles of San Francisco." So the next day we drove to the Napa Valley and had the best lunch at the Napa Grill.

We drove on to San Francisco and across the Golden Gate Bridge. It was a perfect weather day, about 70 degrees and sunny. We drove to within a few blocks of Pier 39, where there are lots of shops and restaurants, and parked our car. Then walked to the pier and watched several boats sailing on the San Francisco Bay. We decided to get some ice-cream cones. After we finished our cones, I calculated the time it was in Tokyo and thought it might be a good time to call Amy.

As we walked to a bench away from the crowds, I felt my phone vibrate in my pocket. It was Amy calling us! Perfect timing.

It was a FaceTime call, so I held my phone up to show her the boats and the pier. She said they looked beautiful! Then she told me that Dillon's grandfather, Howie, had passed away at ninety-two years old in Connecticut. Dillon was very sad because Howie had been like a father to him in his teen years. Howie and his wife, Gram, taught Dillon about golf. Dillon still enjoys this game as exercise and a way to have fun.

Amy said that Zach and Matthew were a real comfort to Dillon now. She added that their family would go to a memorial service for Howie when the family had one later in Connecticut. I told her how sorry we were about Howie and that we would pray for them. She said, "I love you," and so did we. God, please comfort their family at this sad time.

Steven, Jay, and I ate dinner at the Pier 39 Market restaurant and then drove back to our hotel. The next morning, Steven drove back to Oregon, and we drove toward Bakersfield and then to I-40 all the way back to Georgia, which would take a few days.

We heard on the news that on Monday, October 9, a massive wildfire began in the Napa Valley region of California. It was supposedly started by a downed transformer on some power lines. Since we had just been in Napa about a week before, we knew how dry the trees and grasses were. As of October 11, twenty-eight people had died in the fire and 170,000 acres burned. Such a beautiful part of California totally gone. The news report said the fire was like a storm that rolled through the neighborhood at 1:30 a.m., so many people died in their sleep. We prayed that God would help the people who survived.

CHAPTER 11

Dinner in Tokyo and Sports Day at School

Amy and Dillon at La Tour Daikanyama in Tokyo.

In mid-October, Jay and I went to dinner with friends. As we were leaving the restaurant, I saw a message from Amy that said, "I'll call you after I take the boys to the bus stop," to which I replied, "That's good! We will be home in an hour." We had to get gas in our car and pick up a few groceries at the store.

After we got home, I called Amy back on FaceTime. It was so good to see her face. She told us her family had gone to a staff dinner at the Tokyo American Club that evening with a few of Dillon's coworkers including his boss, Azuma-san, and a coworker Fujiki-san. Zach and Matthew asked if they could just walk around the club while the adults had their dinner if they had to go to the meal. Amy said that they were going to the dinner with them. The boys said, "Awww." They are so cute!

Amy said she told Zach to watch for Matthew after school so that they could ride the right bus to go to the Tokyo American Club instead of the one to their apartment. Zach had his own cell phone since he was eleven years old. Matthew was only eight and didn't have a phone yet. Zach used his phone to communicate with Amy and Dillon while he was at school.

Amy said Dillon told her his coworkers to going to speak to her only in Japanese so she could practice her knowledge. They will call her Amy-san and bow when they meet her. Amy said that she had only had five Japanese lessons so far and may not be ready to do this. But I think she will do fine. After her first lesson, after all, she had to take a taxi from the school to their apartment, and she was able to give the taxi driver directions in Japanese.

I said she could make a joke that Dillon was her shugine,

which means master in Japanese. But she said Dillon had already tried that at work, and the Japanese didn't understand sarcasm or innuendo. For example, someone sent him a memo to send suggestions about nice upscale restaurants in Tokyo. Dillon said, "What about Subway?" as a joke. The worker said they would add, "Sub-e-way." Ha ha. Upscale sandwiches.

Amy loves the food in Tokyo. One afternoon she went to a sushi restaurant that had different kinds of sushi on a conveyor belt. You took a plate of each kind of sushi you wanted and then paid at the end. One time she paid $6.95 for lunch.

By the way, the dinner at the Tokyo American Club went great!

Amy told us that Matthew had a sports day at his school later in the week. All the kids played games outside. Amy asked if parents could come, and they said yes. When she got there, Matthew saw her and said, "I didn't know you were coming."

Matthew's friend Kian said, "Your Mom is here," and they both giggled. They had fun. Amy had fun too.

Zach went on a field trip with his sixth-grade class to a nice campground for three days and nights. Amy said the kids were not allowed to have cell phones, but the teachers and chaperones would have their cell phones if needed.

Zach told me that the kids hiked and had fun exploring during the day. At night he slept on a futon. I told him that Jay and I had a futon in our first apartment, and we also used it as a bed when we had company. Zach thought that was neat.

Amy said that after Zach got home from his trip, he

had the weekend off, and Monday and Tuesday were school holidays. Dillon had Monday off too.

Just an aside, Jay and I went to Chattanooga to eat and shop that weekend. I saw a few signs that were thought-provoking. One church sign asked, "Does Heaven Have Rules? Sermon October 15."

That is a very interesting question, one I'd never actually thought about. But my initial answer is yes because without rules, there is chaos. And as God reminded me, Lucifer was cast out of heaven because he wanted to make himself equal to God and have his own rules.

Another church sign read, "All kings of the earth shall praise You, Lord." That is so true. Every king, every president, every ruler will bow down to Jesus. Amen!

CHAPTER 12

Japanese Lessons, Music Lessons and More Speeches

On October 19, 2017, Amy called and said that she was studying her Japanese lesson at a Tokyo coffee shop. For her next class, she had to be able to say a hundred sentences in fifteen minutes. When she told us how the class went, she said she was able to say the hundred sentences in ten minutes. Wow! She even posted a short video about her lesson on FB. It was amazing. She's learning the Japanese language so fast! In 2020, after Amy and her family returned to the United States, Dillon told us that she had done so well and learned the language so quickly that she astonished her teachers.

That was no surprise to us. Amy has always been able to accomplish whatever she was determined to do. From being co-valedictorian of her senior class in high school to making all As in each class at the University of Georgia all four years, to passing the South Carolina CPA exam with flying colors! We're so proud of her. May God bless her with many more happy moments.

Amy had a PTA meeting that week in a lovely home in Tokyo. The home located in an area called Yoyogi Uhara, so she had to take a train. She said the train was so full of passengers that she had to push her way into the train car. Her backpack got caught in the door of the train when it closed. So when she got to her stop, the door would not open. A few people tried to help her get untangled, but a train worker had to come and unlock the door before it would open. Amy said that the train was delayed four minutes. That is a long time in Japan because they are very strict about being on time.

When Jay, Steven, and I were in Europe and England in 2018, we rode many trains. The train schedules were adhered to very closely because so many people depend on them for their transportation. It was a wonderful way to meet people and view the beautiful countryside!

A few days later, Amy FaceTimed us. We were talking about Zach's school, and in the background, I saw Zach setting up for some clarinet practice. He was putting his clarinet together, just like Amy used to do when she played in high school. I told him, "That looks familiar. I bet your mom is able to help you with your clarinet."

Amy said, "Zach is getting pretty good, but I'm still faster." Probably from experience.

Zach started playing a tune on his clarinet. "Sounds like 'Merrily We Roll Along,'" I remarked.

Zach said, "That's right, Mimi."

I was happy about that. "I guess I can still remember songs when I have to."

Soon Matthew came from his room and stood behind Amy, who was sitting on the couch. He said, "I want to video chat with my friend Kian, but Kian's mother says he can't do that until they finish all their homework." And Matthew needed Amy to help him with his homework. So we said goodbye and, "I love you."

I am so glad that Amy is a good mother, able to help Matthew and Zach, and to be there at the apartment when she is needed. What a blessing!

A couple days later, Amy called and said they needed prayers for Zach because he had another speech. This time it was about the periodic table in his science class. Zach was supposed to talk about sodium, Na. I told him it was a good element to talk about because it is interesting since so many adults have to reduce the amount of sodium in their diets for heart health.

Zach said he already knew many facts about sodium, including that sodium, Na, plus Cl is sodium chloride, or salt. I told him that I had made a sign for a speech that I had to give in college at Furman University during my senior biology seminar class. The sign said, "Stop the cloning," because my speech was about cloning, which was a new concept in the 1970s. I had doubled up a towel and placed it on my stomach under my dress; girls mostly wore dresses, not pants, to classes at the time. It looked like I was pregnant. When I walked into the classroom, everyone started laughing. My professor loved it! Later he told me that he was so surprised I did that and was so impressed with my presentation that he gave me an A! I don't even think he heard a word I said during the speech because he was so surprised with the wow factor of the sign and the dress.

I also learned a speech technique from watching *Good Morning America*. A young female entrepreneur who had been a guest on *Shark Tank* said that she does something to embarrass herself in public at least once a day so she can laugh at herself without it hurting her feelings. That's good advice for anyone.

The next day, Amy called and said Zach had an amazing day at school, and his speech went well. Thank You, Jesus! I know that one day Zach is going to be a great public speaker, and all this is in preparation for his future. God bless you, Zach, in all you do. I love you!

CHAPTER 13

Friends Visit, and Foreign Enemies scare

On October 31, Amy sent us a picture of Matthew in a black costume with a plastic horse's head. He looked very tall. Zach decided not to wear a Halloween costume since he was older. They went to the concierge desk at their apartment building, and the young lady at the desk gave them some candy for Halloween.

In Tokyo, there is a big Halloween celebration near downtown, in the Shibuya area. Amy and Dillon's close friends Loren and Christy were visiting from Texas, so they all went to Shibuya to see the festivities. It was like Times Square in New York City. They had so much fun!

The next day, I accidentally touched the screen with Amy's phone number, and Zach answered the FaceTime call with a smile. In a few minutes, Amy was there and asked, "Did Zach tell you that he caught two fish?" I told her no, so she told me they had gone to a river and rented bamboo fishing poles. Zach caught two fish. Dillon took both fish off the hook and returned them to the river. Amy later posted a video of Zach catching the fish. It was cool!

Amy said their friend Loren had found a hotel in another area of Japan for all of them to spend time during the weekend and go sightseeing. They rented a Honda minivan too. The pictures were beautiful.

Amy turned her phone around so we could see everyone. Everybody looked so happy! I showed them Chubbs, who was still living with us. Then we said goodbye and, "I love you and miss you!"

On November 4, 2017, the UCLA men's basketball team was supposed to play the Georgia Tech men's team in China. A few days before the game, three of the UCLA players had gone shopping at a Louis Vuitton store in China. A surveillance video from the store showed that they had shoplifted items like pocketbooks, and so on. They were arrested and held in jail for three days, until negotiations between the US government and China were resolved. The charges against the players were reduced, and the players were allowed to come home.

One of the UCLA basketball players I saw interviewed after they returned said, "I want to thank President Trump and the US government for helping to get us released. I can tell you 110 percent that I will never do something like this ever again." The three players were suspended for ten games and had to earn their way back on to the team. They are all very fortunate and blessed to be out of prison and back home. It is a lesson learned the hard way. Never steal! Especially never steal from a place in a foreign land. Their governments are very strict, and it could have meant ten years in a foreign prison. But God protected them. Thank You, Jesus!

CHAPTER 14

A Different Kind of Thanksgiving: Their First Thanksgiving in Japan

In 2017, a couple of weeks before Thanksgiving, I sent Amy a picture of my dad, Papa Joe, to her since he's her only surviving grandparent. He was wearing the new jacket we had bought him while Jay and I were in Florida visiting him in the nursing home there. Daddy's nurse/caregiver had suggested he needed a good fleece jacket so he could go out. Jay and I went to a local store and found a nice one.

Amy called me back on FaceTime, and we talked for a good while. While we were on the call, she showed me Dillon, who was sitting at the table with his laptop. He was waiting for a conference call to begin. And he was wearing a light-blue dress shirt at 8:00 p.m. Tokyo time. Amy told me that most nights he works so late he just lays on the bed in his clothes and goes to sleep after he's done with his work calls.

All of Dillon's hard work is paying off because his

company, EY, has passed the first phase of winning a global contract. And it's due to Dillon's efforts that they can even bid on it.

A few days later, Amy posted, "Dillon's morning commute," a photo of dozens of people swarming toward the entrance of the subway, with Dillon right in the middle of it all.

She shared that people worked so many long hours that they just lay their heads down on their desks and took a nap whenever they get tired.

Praying for rest for Dillon. God give him strength and rest.

At the end of the call, Amy was putting clothes in the dryer from the washer. "It's good to see you doing daily tasks and smiling," I told her. God bless you, Amy, as you take care of your family!

That Friday, we drove to Atlanta to pick up Steven at the airport. He flew from Portland, Oregon to Denver then to Atlanta. It took us three hours to get back to Summerville because of construction on I-75. When we got home, we were all hungry. Since I had made a pumpkin pie that morning, I cut a piece for each of us and topped them with Cool Whip. At 2:35 a.m. on Saturday, we all had dessert. It tasted great!

A few days later Amy called us again and said that Zach and Matthew were off school for the next week and had asked what they were going to do for Thanksgiving. She told them Dillon was going to take all of them to Kyoto, which is about four hours from Tokyo by train. Matthew asked, "Aren't we going to have turkey?"

Zach added, "We're used to going to Mimi's house and having turkey and pumpkin pie."

Then they both said, "We want to have a regular traditional day."

"Even though we're going to Charlotte for Christmas, we want to have a Christmas tree too!" Amy said they want all the traditional things, even though they're in Tokyo. And the boys are not going to let her out of this one.

God help them to have a good Thanksgiving. It won't be the same here without them.

On Thanksgiving Day 2017, I woke up early to prepare the dressing for the turkey so that it could be put in the oven by 11:00 a.m. I had already told Amy that we would call her at 5:30 p.m. EST, which would be 7:30 a.m. Friday in Japan. They would be in Kyoto for a family vacation since Dillon was off work, and the boys were out of school.

Steven had been home since November 16 but and had gone to Nashville for a few days to be with his married friends, Mayne and Elisa and Luke and Corrine. He also saw several of his running friends at the Flying Monkey marathon race on Sunday and at the Nashville Running Company (NRC) on Monday. He also got to run with his friend, Jeff Davis. Steven came home on Tuesday for Thanksgiving.

On Thursday, Jay's sister, Kitty, came with her husband, Tommy. Since her specialty is baking, she brought a delicious German chocolate cake. Jay's brother, Louis, and his wife, Sue, came from their home in New Orleans. They hadn't been here in several years because Sue has severe back problems. Louis walked her through our front yard and up the two steps to our front door. When Sue and Louis got inside, Sue seemed very happy to be here. And she told us that Jay and I still looked the same.

Not long later, our nephew and his wife, Robbie and Natalie, came from Marietta. They brought their seven-year-old daughter, Adair, and their newborn daughter, Ryla. Ryla was born November 4 and weighed five and a half pounds at birth. She still seemed very tiny to us. I had put our rocking chair near our piano so that I could rock her after dinner.

For now, I went into the kitchen, finished cooking the side dishes, and arranged everything buffet style on the counter. Then I called everyone into the kitchen. Jay said a prayer and thanked God for the food and all who were there, and for Amy, Dillon, Zach, and Matthew in Japan. Then we fixed our plates and ate a delicious meal.

After we finished, it was close to 5:30 p.m. and I FaceTimed Amy. She got to see and speak to everyone. It was great!

The next day, I found out that Amy had to eat cold sushi for her Thanksgiving meal since all the restaurants were full. But good news, she and her family finally got to eat the traditional Thanksgiving meal after church on Sunday at the Tokyo American Club. Hooray! Prayers answered!

Of course, our Thanksgiving in Georgia was wonderful, but I told Amy, "It was good, but it won't be the same until you all are back with us again for Thanksgiving. I love you!"

CHAPTER 15

A Different Kind of Christmas

The good news was that Amy, Dillon, Zach, and Matthew were coming to the United States for Christmas in December 2017. We planned to meet in Charlotte and stay with Amy's friends.

The unexpected news came on December 10. I received a call from my brother, Joel, that my dad had passed away that morning in the nursing home. I texted Amy and told her. She said she would call me as soon as it was morning in Japan. When she called, I told her that Papa Joe had passed away during the early morning hours, and his memorial service would be at the National Cemetery in Sarasota, Florida, on Tuesday. Amy told me that her flight from Tokyo to the United States was scheduled to leave on Tuesday of the next week, but she was going to try and get the flight changed to Sunday, so she could be with us for my dad's service.

It took three days of Dillon talking back and forth with the EY travel service and many prayers, but Amy called on

Thursday and said she had gotten a flight from Tokyo to Tampa on Sunday, December 17. Praise the Lord! I cried when I heard this good news.

I told her I had two scenarios in my mind of the memorial service. One was for just Jay and I to drive to Florida. The other was for Amy to be with us there. Of course, to me, that was the best option.

When Amy emailed me her new flight schedule, and I noticed the travel agent had addressed Dillon as Dillon-san and Amy as Amy-san, a polite form of address in Japan. So I said, "Thank you for the flight information, Amy-san. I love you."

She replied, "I love you, too, Mama-san."

So very precious!

Amy will be flying into the Tampa airport on Sunday, December 17. We will leave on Sunday afternoon for Florida and spend the night in Perry, Georgia. We will drive to Tampa on Monday and pick her up at the Marriott Hotel near the airport. I am so happy that she will be with us at the memorial service in Sarasota on Tuesday.

As it turned out, it was all for the best that she flew into Tampa rather than Atlanta. There was a major power outage at the Atlanta airport for several hours that evening.

We met Amy in Tampa at noon. It was so good to see her again! We put her suitcases in our car and drove to Bradenton. We stayed at the Lakewood Ranch Holiday Inn, which was just a few blocks from our parents' house in Rosedale. My brother and his family stayed there also, so it was good to be able to visit with them several times during the few days before the memorial service.

Tuesday morning, we got up, ate breakfast, and dressed

for the service. We drove down I-75S to the Sarasota exit and turned left toward the cemetery. It was a beautiful day, 75 degrees and sunny. A volunteer on a motorized cart was at the gate. He suggested we go to the left and look around the grounds since we were there early. So we drove around and parked to the left. Then we took pictures of the graves, which had pine wreaths with red bows on each marker. It was so beautiful!

We also took pictures of the Navy Veterans memorial, a glass structure with windows that looked like wings. It is a tribute to all navy veterans, including my dad.

We next drove to the right and were directed to line up our car with others going to my dad's graveside service. I met two couples who had been friends of our parents and shared a monthly get-together with them in years past. Several friends from their church were also there.

When it was time, we drove in the procession to the graveside service area. When we parked and got out of our car, I saw several navy officers and other military officers in full dress uniforms.

A young female naval officer in a white dress uniform approached me and asked, "How are you doing today ma'am?" I said that I was doing well and asked her how she was. She said she was well and that it was an honor to escort me today. She had been told that I was the oldest child of the family. I put my right arm through her left arm, and we walked to the bench in front of the casket. I thanked her.

Amy came and sat on my left, and Jay sat on Amy's left. Two sailors in white dress uniforms took the American flag off my dad's casket. They folded it in half, then in half again, and then in triangles until it was one perfect triangle. One of the young sailors took the flag in his arms, stood in front of me, and said, "On behalf of the President of the United States and the US Navy, we honor his service."

He gave me the flag. Then he took off his right glove. This was a sign to the other sailors that what was coming next was "off script." He turned back to me and knelt right in front of me. Of course, by that time I had tears running down my face. Then the sailor looked directly in my eyes and said, "Thank you for your father's service to our country. Thank you for letting us be a part of this today. It is an honor to be here."

I looked at him and said, "Thank you. God bless you in everything you do."

I knew something special was happening because I had chills all over. What a wonderful ceremony!

God bless that young man and all who serve our country!

After the memorial service, Joel and Cherry were on their way to Pensacola to see their daughter, Rachel, and her family for Christmas. We drove Amy to the Tampa airport because she was flying to Connecticut to meet Dillon, Zach, and Matthew, who were flying there to see Dillon's family before going to North Carolina for Christmas.

On the way to the Tampa airport, we stopped for lunch at our favorite restaurant, the Beach House, near Bradenton Beach. We sat at a table under an awning on the beach. The weather was beautiful, 80 degrees and sunny. We even saw a sailboat on the water in front of us. We got Amy to the airport in plenty of time for her flight. We knew we would see her in Charlotte in a few days. It was so wonderful to have her with us.

When Dillon, Zach, and Matthew flew into LaGuardia

Airport in New York City, who did they see walking through the airport but one of their best friends, Brad, who is a pilot for Jet Blue. God's timing is perfect!

By December 22, we were all at Brad and Kristen's home in Charlotte for Christmas. We had a great time staying at their house. Among the fun things we did were eating dinner at Kristen's mother's house and a girls' spa day, where we got our nails done. And a shopping trip with Kristen, Amy, and Jennie Hopper with her ten-year-old daughter, Grace. We went to a nice clothing store having a sale on boots. Jennie and her daughter tried on several pairs and discovered they both now wore size 7. Kristen bought a shirt for Grace that says, "Amazing Grace," on it. I bought a pair of black suede boots and a pillow that has, "Great is thy Faithfulness, Lord unto me," embroidered on it. I see it every day in our house. Thank You, Lord, for Your faithfulness, new every morning.

We also got to see Zach play in a scrimmage soccer game with his Charlotte friends. He scored a goal! Even some of the fathers played in parts of the game. It was fun getting to see everyone again!

Christmas Day was fun! Brad cooked a great French toast breakfast. Then Kristen's parents, Jim and Mary, came. Brad's brother was there from Atlanta, and his mother came from Winston-Salem. We had a nice dinner together too.

In the evening, we kept our annual tradition of going to the movies on Christmas Day. We went to see *Star Wars: The Last Jedi*. It was a good day!

The next day, Kristen, Amy, and I went shopping at Versona, tried on clothes, and bought a few things. It was fun.

Then we met Mary, Kristen's mom, at a deli and ate lunch together. It was so nice to have a mother-daughter lunch.

Jay, Steven, and I went back to Georgia on Saturday. Steven would fly back to Oregon from Atlanta. Amy and her family would fly back to Japan from Charlotte in a couple days. Amy, Dillon, Zach, and Matthew waved goodbye to us as we left the driveway.

We would not see them until next summer. Godspeed until we meet again!

CHAPTER 16

Zach's Twelfth Birthday, 2018: His First in 2018

Zach, Jack and Matthew and US flag.

Z ach's birthday is on March 15. I texted Amy a few days before and asked about the best time to call him. She said that between 6:30 and 7:00 p.m. Tokyo time would be best since Zach now had track practice after school and got home around 5:45. So Jay and I called Zach at 5:40 a.m. Georgia time, which was 6:40 JST.

Since it was a FaceTime call, it took a few minutes for Zach to answer. It was so good to see his smiling face! We told him, "Happy Birthday." He turned his phone to show us all the food Amy and Dillon had gotten him for his family party. I had bought his favorite cake-like, icing-covered cookies at Walmart, which had green icing with sprinkles on them. We shipped them the week before, so they would be there in time for his birthday. These cookies are wonderful to ship because they taste like cake, have a long expiration dates, and don't fall apart during shipping. When Zach and Matthew saw those cookies, they always got so excited. Amy said they had to have one cookie after they ate breakfast. And then they had her pack a cookie in each of their lunches to have at school.

Zach had tried out for the middle school track team a few weeks ago and made it. So he had practice after school on his birthday. I asked him how it went. "It was hard because they made me run a lot." But he looked happy, so it seems to be agreeing with him. I told him that he would probably sleep well tonight since he exercised so much today.

I also told him that it was snowing on the day he was born, March 15, 2006. Zach said, "Really, It was snowing?"

"Yes. Papa Jay and I got there the day after you were born in Stamford, Connecticut, because it snowed the whole way there from Georgia." I told him his dad was wearing blue scrubs when we arrived at the hospital and got to see

Zach for the first time. Zach was the largest baby in the nursery, weighing nine pounds. Amy had an emergency C-section because the doctor had estimated Zach's weight at about seven pounds the week before and didn't expect him to be so big.

This was his twelfth birthday, and he was so proud of the cake that Amy made him. It was white cake with homemade chocolate icing. Then Amy told us how she found the ingredients. She went to a store in Tokyo called The Food Show and saw a Betty Crocker cake mix, so she bought it. Then she couldn't find icing, so she bought chocolate, butter, and powdered sugar to make it from scratch. Zach showed us her finished, cake and it looked really good.

Zach was really proud of his cake, cookies, and gifts! He said he would open his gifts after dinner. For dinner Amy was going to make tacos for him, his favorite! Zach said that would have a party with his friends in a couple weeks. They plan to eat dinner at a nice restaurant and go to an arcade in Shibuya-ku. That sounds fun!

Zach has a best friend in North Carolina named Jack. They have had their birthday parties together since they were two years old since Jack's birthday is one day before Zach's. Zach told us he talked to Jack today. And since JST is thirteen hours ahead of EST, they had their birthdays on the same day! Jack told Zach that it was snowing in North Carolina.

I hope Zach and Jack will be good friends all their lives. This year they will celebrate their birthdays in the summer, when they're together in North Carolina.

Jack wrote this poem for his class about a life event that meant a lot to him after Zach left for Japan in 2017.

Gone
Friends for 10 years,
All gone in a second.
My eyes, full of tears,
Never to see them again, we reckoned.
Hours of FaceTime
Until the next summertime.
They come to visit during the summer,
him and his brother.
It wasn't lame,
But it definitely wasn't the same.

I made reservations for our annual family vacation at Litchfield Beach in South Carolina during the first week of August. Steven is planning on being there too. He says he may have to have some training runs there because it will be three weeks before his 100-mile race in France, the UTMB-Ultra trail du Mont Blanc. Jay and I are making plans to take the Cunard Line *Queen Mary II* to Southampton, England. Then we plan to take trains to Paris and Chamonix, where the race starts and ends. With God's grace we hope this will all happen in God's timing!

Jay is a part of a wonderful singing group in Georgia called The Sons of Jubal. One of their songs is "God's Faithful Love." Here are some of the lyrics:

Ever seeking, ever changing,
Grace that covers all my weakness,
Constant hope that knows no end.

God's faithful love.

We depend on this love every day. We also depend on His providence.

Amy told me two stories of God's provision that happened the day before Zach's birthday. Zach and Matthew had already left for school on the bus. Zach loves Krispy Kreme doughnuts, so Amy decided to walk to the nearest Krispy Kreme store. When she got there, a long line of men waiting to purchase doughnuts.

Then she saw a sign that said, "March 14th = White Day." She remembered that in Japan, White Day is a designated day for men to buy sweets for their favorite ladies. (February 14 is the day women buy sweets for their favorite guys there.) By the time she reached the store, it didn't have any of the doughnuts Zach likes. Amy went to several more stores and finally found a small package of powdered donuts at a 7-Eleven store. She texted Dillon at work and told him what happened.

Dillon had a late work/dinner meeting after he finished at his office that lasted until 10:30. After that, he took a taxi to the nearest Krispy Kreme store. He got there at 10:45, fifteen minutes before closing, and bought a dozen doughnuts. Dillon placed the donuts on the kitchen counter and went to bed.

The next morning, Zach's birthday, Amy woke up, went into the kitchen, and saw the Krispy Kremes! She ran to the bedroom and asked Dillon how he got them. He explained what he did, and she responded, "It's a Christmas miracle!"

I told her that Jay and I always say, "It's the gift of the

magi," when we give each other similar gifts or something really good happens on a birthday or other special occasion. Amy said that she remembers seeing the movie *Gift of the Magi* when she went to Pennville Elementary School. She has always had a good memory and remembers details. Especially like lyrics of songs she learned in Sunday school and vacation Bible school. And poems she learned in Trion School in the 1980s. That's probably helped her when she studied languages like Japanese and Spanish.

Speaking of miracles, which I call God's providence or divine appointments, some think of them as coincidences. I don't think anything that happens is coincidence. Rather, they are known by God and meant to be beneficial to encourage us or teach us in some way.

For example, when Jay and I took Zach's birthday package to the Trion Post Office, we saw our friend Mrs. Jack Richardson, and said, "Hello! Even though it's March, it's still very cold."

She turned around and started to recite a poem she had learned a long time ago: "When March winds begin to blow, then it's time for snow." It was like a breath of fresh air.

Then one of Amy's favorite teachers from high school, Johnny Brimer, walked into the post office. He asked, "How is Amy doing?"

I said, "We're mailing her a package right now. She always says she's sorry that it costs so much to send something to Japan. We're glad to do it."

Johnny said, "That's just like her, to be thinking of others before herself." It wasn't a coincidence that we saw one of her high school teachers from when we were mailing that package to Japan. God knew we needed encouragement that day, and He sent it! God bless you, Johnny!

God, help us to make it through these long months before we see Amy and her family again. Thank You for Zach and his wonderful birthday. I am so glad he was happy with everything!

CHAPTER 17

Matthew's Tenth Birthday

April 20, 2018 was the day before Matthew's tenth birthday in the United States. Since Tokyo is thirteen hours ahead of us, Amy texted us around 5:30 p.m. and asked if we wanted to be included on FaceTime when she, Dillon, and Zach woke Matthew for his birthday surprises. Of course, we said yes.

At call time, Jay and I were on our way to Rome, Georgia, to go to my Redmond Medical Center Annual Awards Banquet at the Forum. It was my thirtieth anniversary of working at Redmond (1988–2018). We pulled into a parking lot near the Forum and waited for Amy to call us.

Within a few minutes, she FaceTimed us. We could see Matthew come out of his room and going to the couch in the living room. They had several balloons outside his room. Zach was dressed in his track shirt and shorts since it was Saturday, and he had a track meet later that day. We all sang "Happy Birthday" to Matthew. Then he opened his box of Krispy Kreme doughnuts and took a bite out of a chocolate glazed one.

Amy gave Matthew some presents to open. He got a Minion water bottle, a bobblehead, and some money. He also opened two cat toys for Chubbs because it was her birthday too. He seemed very happy about everything!

We sent a box for Matthew's birthday about eight days before, including cookies with blue icing and cards and toys. Amy texted us later, and said the box came. Yay, it got there on his birthday!

Matthew's party with his friends was planned for the next weekend. Amy spent several hours on her laptop making plans for him and his friends to go to the Trampo-time park in Tokyo. Every child had to have a signed permission form.

A week later Amy sent some pictures of Matthew's party. Matthew and his friends were at an indoor trampoline park with several trampolines. It looked like the kids were having a great time.

I am so thankful that Matthew had a good party and will have good memories of his tenth birthday.

CHAPTER 18

Happenings in the United States in April 2018

The same day that Matthew had his birthday in Japan, multiple events were going on simultaneously around us. Dezirea, one of our friends from our Thursday evening supper group, had a baby boy prematurely the week before. He was going to be okay but had to be in NICU for a while. And our pastor's wife had a baby boy the day before Matthew's birthday.

I received my certificate of my thirty-year anniversary of working for Redmond Regional Medical Center in Rome at the annual awards ceremony. A young friend from the laboratory at Redmond passed away suddenly at the same time the awards ceremony was being held.

Some events are beyond understanding. This last one is still so difficult to comprehend. My friend at Redmond had just gotten home from work and had a toddler at home. She went out of her house to get into her car when the vehicle rolled into her and crushed her against the back wall. Life Flight came to rush her to the hospital. We got word that she was fading fast at the same time we were receiving our awards. It was so surreal.

All of us who had been her friends were at her memorial service. Her two-year-old son wandered through the rooms at the funeral home. We knew he was looking for his mother because she loved him so much, and they had such a strong bond. Every year her sister posts pictures of her young son and says, "Your mom is so proud of you."

We will never understand why this happened, but we must trust that God will keep her son in His care and protection.

Why does God allow bad things to happen to good people? That is a question we can't answer. Prayering for safety and protection and for angels to surround you.

> For he will give his angels charge over you,
> to keep you in all your ways. (Psalm 91:11
> NKJV)

CHAPTER 19

Spring 2018 in Japan

A my called on May 3 and told us Dillon had been invited to play golf at a cybersecurity conference in Australia. I guess that's a tangible answer to my prayers about Dillon's health and ways for him to unwind and relieve stress.

While Dillon was away at his conference, Matthew was starting cross-country practice. Matthew is so funny and said that his practice was easier than Zach's track practice because the elementary grade coaches make it fun. The middle school coaches are stricter than the elementary coaches and run the boys really hard. Zach's legs are usually very sore after his practice.

Zach had a track meet this weekend and a band concert on Thursday night. He wanted Amy to pay for a taxi to take them to the concert at the school. But Amy said that it would cost $100, so they were going to walk to the subway and take the train to the school.

Later Amy sent us some pictures and a video of Zach's concert. Zach was standing and playing his clarinet next to two of his friends in the band. He looks so tall. Amy agreed. "You won't believe it when you see him!"

I can't wait! Only about six more weeks. The Fourth of July can't come soon enough! Dear Lord, let us have a good visit with them this summer! Help them to have a safe trip back to the United States.

Thank you for preparing the way for them to come home!

There was more exciting news. In the middle of May, Amy met one of Dillon's work associates who knows the US ambassador to Japan, Bill Haggarty, and his wife, Chrissy. As Amy and this lady were talking, Amy said, "My brother, Steven, lived in Nashville for thirteen years before he moved to Oregon." Since the Haggartys were originally from Nashville, she arranged for Amy to meet them at the US Embassy on May 15.

Amy found a beautiful blue dress with white flowers that looked like colors from a Japanese watercolor painting to wear for the occasion. She went to the embassy and was greeted by Chrissy and her mother. They talked and had a really good time.

Amy and her family were invited back to the embassy on June 28. The ambassador and his family were hosting some other US citizens who lived in Japan for a Fourth of July celebration with food and fireworks. Amy said that it was a fun family day. She wore a red dress to celebrate the day.

Just a note: The previous US ambassador to Japan was Caroline Kennedy. Wow! How exciting.

I am so glad that they're being blessed in Japan! Amy sent us some great pictures of them from the party. Amy looked beautiful in her red dress, and Dillon looked so nice in a navy jacket. He was pointing to a sign that had his company's logo on it. He said EY, Ernst and Young, was one of the sponsors of the event.

Amy and Dillon are already missionaries, and now they are diplomats as well. It's wonderful to see how God is using them for good in Japan. God, bless them in their daily lives and continue to protect them.

CHAPTER 20

Summer 2018

On July 2, 2018, I texted Amy that I was thinking about them and that they would probably be leaving from Tokyo soon to come to the United States for the summer. She texted back that they were packing their suitcases right then and were getting ready for their trip. She texted, "Can't wait, and I love you." Then she added several heart emojis.

Jay and I would be leaving on Wednesday morning, July 4, to go to Charlotte to be with them. By then it was six months since we had seen them in person. FaceTime is great, but there is nothing like being face-to-face with your family and getting to hug them!

This time Amy, Zach, and Matthew were coming to Charlotte first. Dillon would come in about three more weeks.

On July 30, 2018, the plan is tol pick up Steven in Atlanta and drive to South Carolina for a family beach trip. We're so looking forward to being there again!

On July 4, Jay and I drove to Amy's friend, Kristen's house in Charlotte. Amy had told us they were having a cookout there. When we arrived, everyone came outside and greeted us with lots of hugs. Kristen's husband, Brad, was grilling hot dogs and hamburgers. He also had a new smoker, where he was cooking salmon. Kristen had made pimento cheese dip with crackers and watermelon and kale salad. Their friend Jennie came later and brought a delicious corn and black bean salad. Everything tasted so good!

Before we left for North Carolina, I made four dozen cookies, two dozen chocolate chip cookies and two dozen sugar cookies with red and blue sprinkles for the Fourth of July. By the time we left the party, only four cookies remained. Those cookies were a hit!

Jennie said that her children, Aidan and Grace, were staying with her husband, Brad H.'s, parents for a few days. He had just landed in Uganda as a part of his church mission team. Their team was going to minister to a local orphanage and a prison in the area. The mission trip was very successful. The team made friends with many of the local people, and the ladies from the mission group saw that many of the local women had not had new clothes in a long time. So before they left, the ladies with the mission group took out most of their clothes from their suitcases and gave them to the women who worked at the orphanage. You would have thought it was a holiday because the local women were so excited to try on the sundresses and blouses. What a blessing!

Later that evening, we watched neighborhood fireworks from the deck. It was a special day!

We were invited to go on a pontoon boat the next day that Brad and Kristen rented. Since we were staying at a condo and their son Jack had spent the night with us,

Kristen came over in the morning to pick up Jack, Zach, and Matthew so that we could ride with Amy to the lake. We were to meet at Lake Wylie by 1:00 p.m. When we got there, we all got in the boat, and Brad drove us to an inlet that was only about seven feet deep, so we could swim there safely. The kids got in first and were having a great time. Kristen said that I could jump in if I wanted to since the lake water was nice and warm. So I stood on the back side of the boat, held my nose, and jumped in. It felt so good. Kristen threw me a seat cushion, and I floated for a while before climbing the stairs to get back on the boat. We watched Jake ski. Then Brad skied for a while too. After that, Zach and Jack held onto a large, round float as Brad pulled them around. Then Matthew and Jake got on the float and held on while being pulled around the lake.

Soon it was time to go back to the dock and return to our condo. We said goodbye to our friends and went to the condo. We ate delicious sandwiches we made from ham and cheese that we bought earlier at Harris Teeter. Amy ate her favorite cereal. And then we watched some Hallmark Christmas movies since it was Christmas in July on that channel. It's so great getting to spend time with them!

Kristen had scheduled Sunday massages for the girls at the Ballentyne Spa, near her law office. When we arrived at the spa, Kristen and her friend, Jennie H., had already eaten lunch, so Amy and I talked to them for a while. We went upstairs to the patio area when our lunch was ready. I had a delicious roast beef sandwich, and Amy had salmon.

After lunch, we went downstairs and put on fluffy white robes to wait our turns for our massages. When I met the therapist, I told her that I was there with my daughter and her friends and that my daughter and her family were living in Tokyo, Japan. After our massages, the therapist told me to have a good time with my daughter and family. I was so relaxed that I could have floated out of there.

Later I found out that Amy had paid for my lunch and massage. I hugged her and thanked her for a wonderful time!

On Monday, we all went to Kristen's house, while Amy drove to her annual appointment in Winston-Salem. The boys played video games for an hour or so. I asked Kristen what I could do to help her out since she was trying to work from home that day. She said that it would help if I took the boys to the neighborhood pool. So I went upstairs and told them to get ready to go to the pool. Jack, Zach, and Matthew put on their swimsuits and got their goggles and towels together. They were ready in five minutes. I asked Jack if he could take us to the pool on their golf cart, so he it turned around, and we went to the Shannamara subdivision pool. Only a few people were there. I sat on the side of the pool and watched the boys play Marco Polo. They had a lot of fun! After about forty-five minutes, the lifeguard called for "adult swim," and the kids got out of the pool. I had forgotten to bring snacks, but I had some Smarties in my purse, so I gave some to each of the boys. Then they went back in the pool.

One of their neighborhood friends had come to the pool by then. He started playing a color-dunking game with Zach. They hold on to each other, and one guesses what color the other one is thought of. If they guess the wrong color, that person gets dunked under water. They all seemed to have fun!

That evening we were invited to a cookout at Kristen's dad's house. Jim lives in Lancaster, South Carolina, which is about forty-five minutes from Kristen's house. We followed Amy to Jim's house. When we got there, Kristen's mother, Mary, was already there. We were glad to see her. It was an enjoyable time. We had hamburgers, hot dogs, baked beans, coleslaw, brownies, pie, and cookies.

We were leaving for Georgia the next day, so we told them goodbye. Kristen turned toward me and said, "Well I guess this will be the last time I see you for a while."

We hugged, and I told her, "I love you."

God bless Brad, Kristen, Jack, and Jake! They have been so nice to us over the years. Also bless Jim and Mary and their family.

On Monday July 30, 2018, Amy, Zach, and Matthew went to Pawley's Island, South Carolina, to eventually meet us there. Jay and I drove to the Atlanta airport to pick up Steven, who was coming in from the West Coast. Steven's plane was delayed several hours in Dallas on a connecting flight, so we didn't get to begin our trip to South Carolina until 3:00 in the afternoon. There were several periods of heavy rain on our way there, but we finally got to Pawley's Island by 12:15 a.m. Amy and the boys were still awake. They greeted us with hugs and smiles at the door of our condo. It felt so good to get there safely.

Steven's large suitcase was lost during the delay in Atlanta, but the airline had taken down the address of the Litchfield resort where we were staying and delivered the suitcase to the resort office by ten the next morning. So all was well.

The first beach day was beautiful, and we went to the

resort pool with a lazy river and enjoyed a relaxing time there. Amy and Dillon's good friends from Charlotte, Mike and Leah, were staying at the Litchfield with their sons, Drew and Jake, and some of their family. Their sons were the same ages as Zach and Matthew and knew each other from classes at their elementary school, so the boys immediately bonded and began playing games.

We had a great time talking to Mike and Leah. Leah likes many of the same types of books that Jay reads. We told them that we were going to England, France, and Italy in September to meet Steven when he runs in the 100-mile, UTMB race. They told us about their trip to Italy a few years ago and gave us some useful information about Europe.

We had mostly cloudy weather for the rest of the week we had mostly cloudy weather. But we loved it because it didn't get too hot.

On Wednesday we drove to Myrtle Beach, about thirty miles away, to eat dinner at the Sea Captain's House. Amy was so nice to pay for our meal as an anniversary celebration for us since it would be our forty-sixth anniversary on August 5.

On the way back to our condo, we reminisced about Zach and Matthew when they were little boys. About how they would spend the night at our house. I would say their prayers when they went to bed. Then Jay would tickle them and say, "Be very, very quiet." Zach and Matthew would laugh so much!

Zach remembered that when Matthew was two years old, he would pretend not to be able to say, "Papa Jay." He would say, "Shay shay," instead. He also remembered that

I played red light, green light with them. And when I said, "Yellow light," it was time to tickle them. Good memories!

Our last day at the beach, we ate at the local Eggs Up Grill. Zach had asked us if we were going to eat there for breakfast, and I told him yes. This was a tradition started several years ago as a last meal before going our separate ways. This time we would be following each other to our home in Georgia. Steven had gotten permission from Amy's rental car company to help drive her rental car. We had a rest stop at a McDonald's on the east side of Atlanta so that we could take a break and get a snack if needed.

While we were in line at McDonald's, a young man in line behind us began telling Steven that he had just gotten off work, and his boss hadn't been able to pay him yet. He said that he only had two dollars, and he needed food for himself and his brother. Steven said he could get him some food and asked what they wanted to eat. Amy was in line also, near the cash register, and said she would pay for their food. After we all got our orders, Amy took twenty dollars from her purse, gave it to the young man, and said, "God bless you."

The young man said, "There really are good people still around. God is good all the time."

I have never been any prouder of Steven and Amy, and to see Christ in action through our children is awesome!

We got home around 5:00 p.m. Jay unpacked our car, and the boys found some games to play. I knew we still needed some groceries and was going to go get them by myself. Amy asked if she could drive me to Ingles. I told her that it was great to have a wonderful daughter to help me! It was fun shopping, and then we came home and fixed dinner.

The next day was our forty-sixth anniversary! It was Sunday, and we all went to our church together. I taught Sunday school. Amy, Steven, Zach, and Matthew were in my class. Along with Brock, Britton, and Mary.

Amy had asked Sean, our pastor, if she could give a presentation about their experience in Japan during the worship service. She wore a pretty, light-blue and silver brocade dress. She looked so nice. Everyone seemed to enjoy her presentation. Jay had ordered flowers in honor of our anniversary to be placed on the table at the front of our sanctuary. They were beautiful!

After our service, we went home to change clothes and get ready for the cookout we were having with our family. Kitty and Tommy came from Rome and brought a delicious cake. Robbie, Natalie, Addie, and Ryla came from Marietta. We had hamburgers, hot dogs, baked beans, coleslaw, and potato chips. We all had a fun time. God bless our family!

Our last few days of summer 2018 were spent during the first week of August.

As I mentioned earlier, Jay was a member of the men's singing group Sons of Jubal. One of their performances was August 9 at a beautiful church in Snellville, Georgia, a suburb of Atlanta. We wanted Amy, Zach, Matthew, and Steven to get a chance to see them perform. We thought it was perfect timing because they could see the concert and then spend the night with us in a nearby hotel. The next day Amy and the boys could travel to Charlotte to be ready to travel back to Japan.

At first, the weather was great the evening of the concert.

But a thunderstorm soaked all of us as we went out for dinner. Even so, we enjoyed the concert of wonderful music. After they sang, "Holy, Holy, Holy," I told Zach that was a song we would hear in heaven. Another of our favorite songs that year was "He Will Hold Me Fast," which Steven really liked too. He told us that song often ran through his mind when was running. As always, God uses everything for our benefit.

We all spent the night in a hotel. We ate breakfast together in the morning. We waved goodbye as Amy and Zach and Matthew drove off toward Charlotte. Amy held her left arm out the driver's window to wave to us. We stood outside the hotel and waved, knowing it would be several months before we would see them again. Saying goodbye is always bittersweet! But we know God has this under His control. Ever blessing, ever blessed! Help us, o Lord.

From August 26 to October 4, Jay and I took our voyage from New York City to London through France to see Steven on the day after he finished his 100-mile Ultra trail du Mont Blanc race. Three days after he ran 100 miles, all three of us went on a tour bus to Courmayeur, Italy, for a day of sightseeing. Steven took us through the streets that he had come by in this city. There were still paint markings on some of the cobblestones to indicate where the runners were to go on the course. The day was sunny and glorious! Many of the shops and houses had beautiful red geraniums growing in pots out front. We ate delicious real Italian pizza and had gelato at three shops during the day. One flavor of gelato was colored white and blue and called Mont Blanc. At lunch one day, I fed a sparrow a few crumbs from some leftover bread. I thought of the song, "His Eye Is on the Sparrow, and I Know He Watches Me."

After a few more days in Chamonix, we took the train to Paris and spent several days there. From our balcony window, Steven, Jay, and I could see the Eiffel Tower. The Eiffel Tower lights up gradually at night until it's fully bright by about 10:00 p.m. Every day we walked many blocks through the streets of Paris. And we always ate at our favorite restaurant each evening, which was near our hotel. Our waiter was always Kevin, and he spoke English very well.

We went to the Louvre, which has many floors. We saw the *Mona Lisa* and the *Venus de Milo*. We also saw many other beautiful paintings and artifacts. The Louvre used to be the king's palace before Versailles was built and was very beautiful inside.

Our favorite historical site was the Notre Dame Cathedral. As we entered the large wooden doors, beautiful organ music began to play. We discovered that we had heard the beginning of a high mass on Saturday evening. There was a procession of choristers and choir boys with candles. We heard some beautiful solos and saw the rose window near the ceiling.

When we learned that the cathedral burned in 2019, we learned that the rose window remains. We were so blessed to see the cathedral as it had been for centuries.

On Sunday, we took the Eurostar train through the chunnel from Paris to London. The chunnel goes under the English Channel. The train runs at speeds nearing 200 miles per hour, but it doesn't seem that fast. And it was fun for us.

We spent three great days in London. We stayed at

the Lancaster Gate, located just a few blocks from Hyde Park and Kensington Palace. Kensington Palace is famous as the residence of Queen Victoria around the turn of the twentieth century and then Princess Diana in the 1980s and 1990s. When we visited London, Prince Harry and Duchess of Sussex Meghan Markle (as there titles were then) resided at Kensington. We didn't see any royals in person but were on a tour bus when a black car sped by with lights flashing. The driver said that royals were passing us. All history of England is fascinating!

Many more of our experiences are recorded in my book *Steven: A Runner's Life,* which was published in 2020 by Balboa Press and available on Amazon.com.

Steven flew home to Oregon at the end of the week. We took a bus to Southampton and then our ship back to New York City. From there, we drove back to Georgia. It was the trip of a lifetime!

CHAPTER 21

A Seventh-Grade Soccer Season and a Fifth-Grade Miracle

Matthew and his friend.

In October 2018, Zach was in the seventh grade at ASIJ. The middle school soccer team held tryouts for those who wanted to play for the team. The tryouts were after school for two consecutive days, which had the kids doing different drills each day.

After Zach got home from the second day of drills, one of the school's coaches called to tell him he had made the soccer B team. Since the A team was almost exclusively eighth-graders, and Zach had just begun seventh grade, he was happy to make the B team. Amy said he did his "happy dance" around the house when he found out.

We congratulated Zach and wished him good luck with his soccer games when we talked to him on FaceTime. Amy kept us up to date on his progress in his games, which were usually held on Saturdays at a local US air base soccer field. Amy said there were nice benefits to being on a US military base. They were allowed to go to the commissary after the games and shop for grocery items that weren't available in local Tokyo stores. Zach did well in all of his games that year.

We are so proud of you, Zach! We know you're special, and God has set you apart for His good work. Love and prayers for the rest of your seventh-grade year.

Matthew started fifth grade that year, his last year in elementary school. Amy told us that he has several good friends at school, and they look up to him. His best friend this year is Noah.

Each fall semester, most students in the fifth grade go on a retreat in the country outside Tokyo. Some teachers go along as chaperones. They sleep in tents for two nights, cook their own meals, and learn about nature. Canoes available for the students to use on the nearby lake.

The chaperones sent Amy pictures of Matthew while he was there. Amy sent some of them to me. One of the pictures was of Matthew riding a mountain bike. Another was one of him preparing a meal over a campfire. He looked like he was having a good time.

Little did he know that he was going to make a name for himself there. God was going to allow Matthew to be part of a miracle. We learned about the series of events that happened there after Matthew came home.

Noah's mom called Amy and told her that Matthew saved Noah's life. She learned this from one of the teachers who witnessed it all. Then she told Amy the details.

Matthew, Noah, and another boy were in one of the canoes on the lake when Noah had an asthma attack. Matthew saw Noah having trouble breathing and rowed the canoe as close as he could to the shore. Then he got out of the canoe and had the other boy help him pull the canoe, with Noah in it, to the shore. Matthew called to a teacher to help them. She went to Noah's tent, found his inhaler, and brought it to him. Noah was soon able to breathe normally again.

After hearing the story, things started to make sense to Amy. When she unpacked Matthew's suitcase, she noticed that all of Matthew's clothes were wet. When she asked Matthew why, he just said they went in the lake and gave no further explanation.

Sometimes boys are men of few words. Amy was so glad that Noah's mother called her and explained what happened. And to know that because of Matthew's quick thinking, Noah's life was saved! Matthew, we're so proud of you.

Noah's mother was so pleased with Matthew that she sent a large bunch of expensive grapes to their family. Amy explained that in Japan, people send fruit as a way of expressing high appreciation because fruit is so prized.

In our family, we always say, "God bless you," to anyone who sneezes. When Matthew sneezed while staying at our house during a visit from Japan, Matthew told us, "People in Japan don't say, 'God bless you,' when someone sneezes. We have to bless ourselves." Well, Matthew, God has blessed you already as you continue to help others. God has big plans for your life!

CHAPTER 22

Hawaii for Christmas 2018, and a 2019 Birthday Surprise for Jay

In December 2018, Amy FaceTimed us and said she and Dillon had looked at flights to come to the States for Christmas, and they were very expensive. She said they would book their flights for next Christmas earlier, so they would get a better deal.

For Christmas 2018, they were going to go to Hawaii and stay at the Explorer Resort owned by Disney. This resort had many amenities, such as multiple pools and restaurants. But there was no theme park. They had beautiful weather while they were there, with temperatures in the eighties during the day and seventies in the evenings. When Amy called us one day, she was sitting on a lounge chair beside one of the pools, watching Zach and Matthew swim. She said they basically had the whole pool to themselves as no other people were around. It was very relaxing. That evening their family went to a traditional Hawaiian luau and ate delicious food.

The second day, they went to Pearl Harbor to see the remains of the warships there. Dillon was able to play a round of golf too. They had a nice dinner together after they returned to their hotel.

When they returned to Tokyo, Chubbs was so excited to see them. Their housekeeper had come to the apartment every day to feed and check on her.

A week after New Year's Day was Amy's forty-third birthday. When we called her, she told us that Dillon, Zach, and Matthew had all gotten up early and made her favorite breakfast, including homemade hash browns. Amy scanned the apartment with her phone, and we saw Chubbs in her favorite spot—in the living room under the Christmas tree.

We mailed Amy a package with items she likes, such as her favorite coffee, a necklace, and birthday cards. I also included some snacks for Zach and Matthew. Amy was very happy with all the gifts, cards, and birthday wishes from friends and family. We were so glad that she had a good day!

My birthday is five days after Amy's. A few days after that, I began to feel lonely and wished I could see Amy. One day I came home from our ladies' prayer group and started sweeping out our garage to keep busy.

I was also talking to God, telling Him that maybe it didn't seem like a long time to anyone else, but it seemed so long until I would see her in person. The planned time for them to come home for the summer was in late June.

Literally within twelve hours, Amy called me and said that Dillon was going to send her home to Georgia for Jay's seventieth birthday in February. I was so excited! God answered my prayers, and we would see her in a few days, when we picked her up in Atlanta.

Jay's party was great! Amy's good friend Kristen came to see her from Charlotte. Many of our friends and family members came, including my good friend Sherry and her husband, Jerome. Our nephew and his wife, Robbie and Natalie, and their beautiful daughter, Adair came. As did my sister and brother-in-law, Leigh Anne and Stanley. Jay's sister, Kitty, made a delicious cake, and Tommy was there too. And Steven brought his girlfriend, Mallika, from Nashville, who made a butter cake for Jay too. It was great to meet and talk with her! Everyone had such a good time, and it continued at our home in Summerville with lots of good stories and laughter.

God surprised us with Amy coming home and lots of friends and family for a great evening.

During the final week of February, Zach went on a field trip with his seventh- grade class to Hiroshima, Japan, for three days. He sent me some pictures of himself in Hiroshima. He also asked me to help him with a school presentation that he was giving on World War II. He knew that my dad, Zach's great-grandfather, had served in the navy in WWII. I told him a few stories about my dad that he used in his presentation. Zach told me it went great.

More answered prayers.

CHAPTER 23

Spring 2019: More Birthdays, Easter, and Visits from Steven and Friends

Steven and Amy with her family.

On March 15, 2019, Zach had his thirteenth birthday. When we called him on FaceTime, he seemed happy with his birthday presents, which we sent to him by way of Amy's suitcase after Jay's birthday celebration. We sent Zach some Nerf guns, Nike T-shirts, and a box with his favorite iced cookies and Rice Krispy treats. Zach especially liked the birthday card I sent that said, "Happy 13th birthday," and had thirteen dollars inside.

His birthday was on a school day, and Amy and Dillon had purchased some Krispy Kreme doughnuts for Zach's breakfast. Amy said that Zach had invited eight boys to come home with him after school to spend the night. They had all gone to a play at the high school after classes and then came over to Zach's home. Amy cooked steaks for them and had a cake too. She told us the boys had all slept with blankets on their rug. For breakfast she made them waffles on Saturday morning. We were very glad that Zach had a good birthday.

About a week later, Steven flew to Tokyo for a nine-day visit with Amy, Dillon, Zach, and Matthew. Since it was spring break from school in Japan, they all went to Kyoto for a long weekend of sightseeing. Kyoto is one of their favorite cities because of the beautiful architecture and great food. The famous red columns on the front of some temples are symbolic of Japanese culture.

After they returned to Tokyo, they showed him many sights in Tokyo. He loved the many good restaurants. One of their favorite restaurants was La Hacienda, a wonderful Mexican place.

Since Steven is a trail runner, he usually doesn't go too many days without at least a three- to five-mile training run. Dillon suggested he try running around the Imperial Palace, near downtown Tokyo, since he had seen other athletes running there, and the distance was about three miles. Dillon's offices were located in a new building near the palace also.

Steven ran on the road around the palace where the emperor of Japan lives. Then he went into the building where EY has offices and upstairs to see Dillon. Dillon introduced him to his boss and several of his team members. They were very nice.

Steven said he had a wonderful visit. He safely flew back to Portland a few days later. We always pray for safety for any of our friends and family who are traveling. I was so thankful that he got back safely!

On April 6, Amy called, but I talked to Zach first. He told me about his track meet on Saturday. It was a 4 x 400-meter relay race. Amy said Zach ran very fast and helped the team out. The next weekend Zach won his own 400-meter race. He ran track in the spring and played soccer in the fall at ASIJ.

I remember watching the 4 x 400 relays in the Olympics, and one of the hardest things to do is to pass the baton without dropping it or missing a handoff to the next runner on the team. Zach said they practice the handoffs a lot.

Amy said Matthew is doing well in math. He got the highest grade in his class on a math achievement test last week. He also gave a speech in his debate class and did well. We're so happy for Zach and Matthew and all they've accomplished so far.

Amy was getting ready to go to their church, Tokyo First Baptist. It's only a few minutes from their apartment. She showed me her electric curlers, which she's had since she was in high school. They still work, and her hair looked beautiful. Dillon was making sandwiches to take with them since they were going to eat lunch in a park nearby after church.

It was so good talking with them. Love and prayers always.

April 21, 2019 was Matthew's eleventh birthday. It was also Easter Sunday. On our Saturday evening in Georgia, I saw my phone light up and then Matthew's smiling face on FaceTime. Since it was already his birthday in Japan, Jay and I sang "Happy Birthday" to him and asked how he liked the gift box we sent him. He said he really liked the iced cookies, the Nike T-shirt, and the Twizzlers candy. Then he said that Jack, Jake, Brad, and Kristen had come to Tokyo during their school's spring break. Both families had traveled to Kyoto for the weekend to see some of the beautiful sights there.

Amy got on the phone next, and we wished her a happy Easter. She said it was probably the first Easter in her life that she hadn't gone to church because they were in another city.

The next person I saw was Zach. He came into the room with his hair all spiked up just after his morning shower. He was looking for a hairbrush. Then his friend Jack photobombed the call, and we said hi. Amy told us they were getting ready to go out for food and more sightseeing. And that Matthew had his birthday cake yesterday and liked it.

It was so good to talk to them and see them so happy.

Jay joined the Sons of Jubal men's chorus in 2018. Our friends Don and Teresa invited him to join since Don was joining the group also. It's proved to be a great experience for both of us.

Following are a few excerpts from our Sons of Jubal conference that winter.

> The Creator, Master, Savior,
> God the Father, Spirit, Son,
> He's the Alpha and Omega,
> The Almighty One.
> Holy, holy, God Almighty,
> He who was and is to come.
> He's the power and the glory
> God Almighty is …
> God Almighty is.

From Psalm 23:

> Surely goodness, surely mercy
> Shall follow me all my days
> And I will dwell in your house forever
> And bless your holy name
> If I walk through the valley of the shadow
> of death.
> I will fear no evil
> If I walk through the valley of the shadow
> of death
> You are by my side.

CHAPTER 24

Nashville, Oregon, and Litchfield Beach: Family Time

Our family photo at the Fox Cafe in Bend, Oregon 2019.

O n the last Wednesday of June 2019, Jay and I began our second trip to Oregon. Our first trip was in 2017, when we drove there for Steven's Mountain Lakes 100-mile race f to qualify for the UTMB in France.

Our goal was to reach Oregon by Monday, July 2, in order to be in Bend and then to meet Amy, Zach, and Matthew, who were flying in from Tokyo to Portland. Amy rented a car at the Portland airport and would drive to Bend to meet us.

The plan was for us to meet Steven for lunch at the Pharmacy Restaurant in East Nashville, and leave on our way to St. Louis, Missouri, for the first night. We did have a great lunch with Steven, but then our car's service indicator light came on. And due to a cracked radiator in our Nissan during one of the hottest days (above 97 degrees) of the summer, we spent two extra days in Nashville. We stayed at Steven's friends' home since they were on vacation while our car was being repaired. Even if it were repaired in time to meet Amy, we were not certain it was safe to drive our car all the way to Oregon. Amy and Dillon found out about our predicament and generously offered to arrange a rental car for us to use on our trip.

We were finally able to begin our journey out west. Our first day of traveling was fourteen hours of driving to Independence, Missouri. The next day we drove to Colby, Kansas, with a major rest stop in Abilene, Kansas, at the Eisenhower Library, which is one of our favorites.

On this same day, Steven and his girlfriend, Mallika, were leaving Nashville. She had gotten a new job at a hospital in Seattle, and he was helping her drive to the West Coast. They had already packed her furniture in a storage unit to be transported the following week to her apartment in Seattle. They would be meeting us in Oregon July 4.

We finally arrived in Ontario, Oregon, on July 2,2019. The following day, as we were driving to Bend, Amy called and said they were already there and would meet us for lunch at the Victorian Café. When we got to Bend and were on one of the roundabouts near the restaurant, Amy texted us and said, "We just saw you and waved at you, but you passed us." How funny! I was looking down at our GPS and missed seeing them. We looked up and saw Amy, Zach, and Matthew waving. We parked our car and got out. It was so wonderful to see them and know we had arrived at our destination! Steven pulled up in the parking lot too.

Breakfast was amazing. We ate at a table outside, and everyone talked at once. We took some pictures and decided to drive to Steven's A-frame in La Pine and then to our Airbnb, both about thirty minutes away. But first we would go to a movie in Bend to see the latest *Spiderman* and then to Target to get some groceries.

As we went through the aisles of the store, Zach and Matthew and Amy got so excited. They filled a grocery cart with items they hadn't seen in a year, things like napkins, snacks, and Funfetti cake mix and icing. Matthew says it's the best icing. I planned to make a cake for Mallika when she arrived in Bend the next day. She had just found out that she passed her last certification test for high-risk obstetrical anesthesiology. We're so proud of her. What an accomplishment!

On Wednesday, July 4, while Mallika was driving from Idaho to Bend, Zach, Matthew, and I made a cake for her at our Airbnb, which had a kitchen. Our Airbnb was a house owned by Ms. Linda, one of Steven's friends. Steven had stayed there in 2017, before he bought the RV where he lived for fifteen months as he renovated his cabin.

Mallika arrived late Wednesday morning. We decided to eat lunch at our rental house. We made delicious sandwiches and ate cake. It was so fun!

After lunch we went to La Pine Park and hiked to Paulina Falls. Along the way we saw the huge ponderosa pines Oregon is famous for. We took some beautiful family pictures there.

For dinner we went to Bend and ate at one of our favorite restaurants, McMenamins, a family-owned chain of restaurants, historic hotels, and music venues. The one in Bend is a converted Catholic convent and school. It also has an indoor pool. When we ate there in 2017, we saw kids and their parents coming through the outdoor eating area in swimsuits with towels wrapped around them and wondered where the pool was. A waiter told us it was indoors to the right. How cool! We love eating the pizzas there.

And on the way back to La Pine, we saw fireworks. It was, after all, the Fourth of July!

Thursday we decided to go to Crater Lake National Park, which was a couple of hours south of La Pine. When we got into the park, there were so many cars because of the holiday weekend. We parked at a lookout site and took some photos. Then went to the park hotel and sat in rocking chairs on the outside porch, where the view of the lake was amazing.

When we went through the gift shop, Amy saw Josh, one of their close friends from who had moved to Oregon. It was totally unplanned! She called out to him, and he was astonished to see her. Then she saw his children. They all hugged and talked for several minutes. They had decided to go to the park at the last minute while waiting for his wife to come back from visiting her parents. What a divine appointment!

Friday was a relaxing day. We ate dinner at Steven's cabin. Mallika made us delicious spaghetti. On Saturday the "girls" went to Bend to get our nails done. Mallika called us, "the hot women." The guys went to a nearby arcade to play games and get some snacks. Papa Jay went to a local bookstore to find a good used book. We met at a nice shopping center and looked around at Ross while Steven and Mallika shopped at Trader Joes for corn on the cob and Caesar salad to bring to their friend Mike's house later. He lives near downtown and the beautiful Deschutes River.

We had a wonderful time eating there and took a walk by the river after dinner. Then we roasted marshmallows on the firepit in his backyard. It was great.

On Sunday morning, we drove to Steven's church, Westside Baptist, in Bend. It was an uplifting time of praise and worship. Then we went to downtown Bend. Many people were out and about, enjoying the beautiful weather. Steven's good friend Breezy was working a summer job at the Foxtail restaurant, and we decided to get some brunch items there. Breezy is a professional photographer and teaches at the local college during the school year. Steven asked her to take a few pictures of our family before we left. Of course they were some of the best photos we ever had taken.

After lunch we drove up to Pilot Butte, which is an observation point where people can see different mountains in the area. It was formed many thousands of years ago from volcanic eruptions called calderas.

Then it was time to say goodbye to Amy, Zach, and Matthew. They were traveling to Portland for a flight to Charlotte the next morning. We would see them again in a few weeks, at Pawley's Island, South Carolina, for our family beach trip.

Steven, Mallika, Jay, and I drove to Steven's cabin after we went to the last Blockbuster store on the planet, which was located in Bend. Mallika got ready to drive to Portland to visit her cousins. It turned out that she spent the night in Amy's hotel room in Portland after her visit. She drove to Seattle the next day to be there in time for her hospital orientation.

That night we watched the movie Steven rented at Blockbuster. The next day, Steven, Jay, and I drove our separate cars through southwest Oregon and ate lunch at Becky's Café in Prospect. Jay and Steven had boysenberry pie and ice cream for dessert. I had coconut cream pie.

After lunch, we drove south through to the Hiouchi Hotel in Crescent City, California. We had planned to see the Redwood Forest in northern California. The first day we ate at a nearby restaurant and then drove about a mile to walk some beautiful trails and see the redwoods. These forests were the background of the scenery filmed in 1984 for the *Star Wars* movie *Return of the Jedi*. Our family has seen all the *Star Wars* movies. One of our favorite sequences is the speeder race through the forest with Luke Skywalker and the Ewoks.

We had some travel information that showed there was a locally famous lighthouse in Crescent City called Battery Point Lighthouse. We drove to the parking there and walked across the smooth stones that formed the beach toward the lighthouse. We took the tour and went up the stairs. Steven climbed the final ladder to the top; I decided to climb it too. What an exhilarating feeling to be at the top and see for miles out to sea.

That evening we went to a great restaurant we had seen on the way to the lighthouse. They served the best sweet potato fries I've ever eaten. Steven got up early the next day and ran on the trails in the Redwood Forest. We met him for a hike. He made a walking stick for his dad out of a tree limb. We enjoyed our time together as always. The next day we drove toward Half Moon Bay, California and Steven drove his car back to La Pine.

Five days later, we arrived back home in Georgia and discovered that we had no Wi-Fi due to a storm that cut out our internet and TV. And since our screened porch was being renovated to an all-season room, porch furniture was piled in our dining room. Fun problems?

Jay and I had about seven days before we driving to the Litchfield Beach in South Carolina to meet Amy and family. It was only five days until Steven flew to the ATL so that he could go with us to the beach, our annual family tradition for the past eight years. Steven's girlfriend, Mallika, had just begun her new job in Seattle and wouldn't be able to join us. But hopefully she can next year.

We picked up Steven in Atlanta and drove to Pawley's Island. For lunch we went to Lorenzo's Restaurant and had great pizza and salad. Then we drove to the resort to check in to our condo. The resort has a Starbuck's stop to the right of the main lobby and waiting area now. Steven and Jay got some coffee, and Steven bought some mugs. After we got the keys to our condo—four bedrooms/three baths—we unpacked our car.

Before long, Amy, Dillon, Zach, and Matthew arrived. We were so happy to see them! I had bought two baseball mitts and a ball at Target. I gave them to Zach and Matthew, and they began throwing the ball to each other. Steven has always enjoyed playing baseball, and played on many adult teams, so they went outside and threw the ball to Zach and Matthew. I was so glad it was a hit.

That evening we went to Quigleys Restaurant for dinner. We had our family picture taken by a nice couple outside afterwards. We had a wonderful time the next few days, going to the beach and pool every day. It was such a great time together.

After we left Litchfield, we drove back to Georgia. Steven came with us since he would fly back to Oregon from Atlanta in a few days. Amy, Dillon, Zach, and Matthew drove to Charlotte, where they would return to Tokyo for their last year.

We would get to see them in December, when they come back to Georgia for my seventieth birthday celebration and Steven's fortieth birthday at Provinos in Rome, Georgia. Until then, FaceTime would have to do.

Zach will be in eighth grade this school year; Matthew will be in sixth grade. Zach is captain of his middle school soccer team. Matthew runs with the middle school cross country team. He says he's so small compared to the seventh- and eighth-grade boys. He runs so fast, though, and was asked why he doesn't pass some of the older runners. He said, "Those guys have muscles." One of these days, Matthew, you will be as large as those guys. It's only a test to see what you can do. Just wait for the rewards. Matthew, God is going to take you places you've never imagined.

> How unsearchable are the incredible riches
> of our Lord, How deep how unfathomable
> His ways, His wisdom, His wonder.
> (Romans 13:1–2)

CHAPTER 25

Fall 2019 to Winter 2020

Matt W. and Amy's family at snow wall.

After Amy and her family left for Tokyo and their last year in Japan, I finished the final draft of my first book. *Steven: A Runner's Life* is about Steven's ultrarunning journey. I submitted the manuscript to my publisher and began the process to complete all that they required.

Amy and her family enjoyed their fall and asked if I could plan my seventieth birthday party for December, when they planned to be home for the holidays. I reserved a dining room at Provinos restaurant in Rome for December 20. I also thought we should include a celebration of Steven's birthday since he turned forty on September 20. He could invite a few friends. His girlfriend, Mallika, would be there also.

The was great! Many of our family and friends were able to be there. I had two cakes made, one for myself and one with an icing A-frame cabin and pine trees for Steven's birthday.

After Christmas, Amy, Dillon, Zach, and Matthew went back to Japan for the last few months of their time in Tokyo. Mallika went back to Seattle for her work at a hospital there. Steven stayed in Georgia. He would travel to Nashville to renovate his house in Tennessee before going back to Oregon in January.

Then my first book was published December 17, 2019. When I saw the final cover of my book on my computer, it took my breath away. But when a shipment of my books from Balboa Press came by UPS on December 23 and I was able to hold a book, my joy was complete!

As more and more of our friends and family learned of the book, more opportunities arose. We planned to take some books to Nashville Running Company, where Steven worked for several years and where his ultrarunning adventure began. We went there in early January and saw Lee, the owner, and Beth, one of the crew members on the Bear Lake 100, Steven's first 100-mile race. It was a dream come true to take my book there and put it on a table in the store.

In early March, Pastor Sean told me he wanted our church to have a book signing for me. Then he suggested that I ask Steven if he could be there too. We scheduled it for Saturday, March 14, 2020.

Little did we know the world as we knew it would change on that date.

Steven conferred with Mallika, and they decided he should come to my book signing. With only about six days until the signing, Steven looked at flight schedules from Seattle to Atlanta and then from Seattle to Nashville for the best one to take since the number of available flights was dropping daily due to the pandemic. He determined that the flight to Nashville would pose the least risk to all of us. He would land in Nashville on Thursday evening and take an Uber to his house there. Jay and I would drive to Nashville, pick him up, and drive back to Summerville the next day.

Eighteen months later, it's strange to remember how rapidly conditions declined at the beginning of the COVID-19 pandemic. It was so frightening and real then; conditions seemed to deteriorate by the hour. By the time we got to Steven's house in Nashville, Mallika had texted Steven that he should probably wear a mask in our car to be sure he didn't transmit any possible viruses to us since we were over seventy years old.

We drove back to Summerville with no issues. The next day was my book signing at our Church Family Life Center.

The book signing went so well. Many people came to have their books signed, and others were there to buy books.

We had a beautiful cake prepared by Paula from Sweet P's. And Kitty, Jay's sister, made a cake in the shape of an open book, which was also delicious. Many of our friends were there and had made wonderful chicken salad sandwiches, cheese straws, and so on. It was all so good. Many thanks to Don, Teresa, Amanda, Derek, Maghan, Mary, Robert, Diane. and Mike. And especially to Stephen Peppers for producing a video of our Steven's photos from the book and adding a soundtrack, "Something Just Like This." There was also a beautiful flower arrangement on the table.

But with the good came the unexpected. For the first time, I heard the phrase, "We need to stay six feet apart." Several people could not attend because they already had symptoms of COVID-19. Many who did attend asked, "Are we having a church service here tomorrow?" My book signing on March 14, 2020, was the last public event at our church for several months.

There were so many questions then and many more in the next days, weeks, and months. We will rely on prayer and the promises to us in God's Holy Word, the Bible.

> He who dwells in the shelter of the Most High Will rest in the shadow of the Almighty I will say of the Lord, He is my refuge and my fortress, My God, in whom I trust. Surely He will save you from the fowler's snare And from the deadly pestilence. (Psalm 91:1–3 NIV)

CHAPTER 26

The Quarantine Begins: Steven Stays for Two Months, and Amy and Family Can't Come Home

From my journal:

Here it is, March 31, 2020, the last day of the month, and day 17 of my self-imposed isolation/quarantine. Since March 14, the day of the book signing for my first book—about Steven's ultrarunning journey—I've only gone outside our neighborhood one time.

Last Thursday was my friend Savannah's 23rd birthday. I wanted to take her a birthday card, so Jay took me to the local nursing home where she works. I texted her that we were coming there. She told me to park in the employee parking lot, and she would come outside to meet us. Soon we were at the back entrance, and she walked out the back door with her, "Savannah smile." I got out of the car, gave her the card, and blew her a kiss. No hugs since social distancing was already in place. Savannah is a CNA—certified nursing assistant—and helps take care of many of the residents there. God protect her!

Every day I looked at my Yahoo! weather app, which began listing the number of new positive cases of COVID-19 in each state, city, or county. The main cities I check daily are Summerville, Georgia; Portland, Oregon; and Tokyo, Japan. On this day, March 31, 2020, there are 1,007 positive cases in Georgia out of 3,815 total cases. In Tokyo there are 87 positives in Japan out of 1,953 total cases.

Amy told us they have decided to self-quarantine in their apartment and only go out for groceries once a week. Dillon is working from home, and Zach and Matthew are doing school from home. Amy told us that many people in Tokyo were going to the local parks and in groups outside, but their family was going to stay isolated from that.

Later, I went with Jay to get gas in our Honda Civic so that Steven would have enough gas to make it all the way to Nashville without stopping the next day. I felt like we were almost doing something against the rules, but we didn't get close to people and came home right after we filled up the car.

Steven was going to Nashville tomorrow to begin some minor repairs at his house there. Amazingly, he sold his house during the height of the pandemic, and he needed to go over a list of items to be fixed before the closing. We knew that God was responsible for this sale, and it made us feel good that Steven came for the book signing, and having to stay extra weeks, this sale was a welcome bonus.

Praying for the right decisions to be made and the cost of repairs will be reasonable.

Now it's Wednesday, April 1, 2020. I only saw one potential April Fool's joke that I thought was funny, and it was posted by a local parent. He said, "I'm going to set my alarm for 6:30 a.m., and then tell my kids that it's time to get up and get ready for school. Then say 'April Fool!' and watch their reactions.

Later today, the governor of Georgia announced that schools would be closed for in-school learning for the rest of the school year. That's really disappointing for so many!

Also, the governor said that a shelter in place rule starts this Friday, April 3. It's only to protect us and keep us safe since it's one of the ways to keep this virus from spreading. Lord help us.

Steven left our house for his house in Nashville this morning at 7:30a.m. He texted me at 10:30 a.m. EDT to let me know that he got there safely. He will be talking to a contractor who will be doing some of the repairs on his house. Then he talks with an electrician who will come do those repairs soon.

I sent lots of good food with Steven when he left our house—chili, cubed steak and gravy, peas, rice, rolls, and cake. He should have plenty to eat while he's in Nashville. God protect him while he's there and when he travels back home.

CV numbers posted for Georgia today were 765 positives out of 4,694 total cases. Good news from Seattle and Washington State, where Mallika is currently working as an anesthesiologist at a hospital there. CV cases decreased to 382 positives out of 5,305 total cases today. She didn't have to work today since she was on call yesterday. She had breakfast with a friend and got her front tire repaired at

Costco for free since she had purchased it there a few weeks ago, and it was still under warranty. When she did take call, she was able to rest for a few hours because no new cases came in. We're praying for her to be protected from the virus and to get enough rest.

Lord, let this virus pass by us as in the days of the first Passover in the Bible, when the Hebrews coated the doorposts with the blood of a lamb. Amen.

Thursday, April 2, 2020. Our governor has ordered a shelter in place for all Georgia residents beginning Friday at 6:00 p.m.

We were still able to have tradespeople come into our home for repairs and upkeep. Tri-state Appliance came and changed out the icemaker in our refrigerator that had stopped working. Two young men wore masks and took only 10 minutes to change it. They both said, "Have a blessed day," when they left. Same to you both!

Our "bug man" for over 30 years, Jessie, came this morning to do his monthly inspection and fumigating. The first thing he said to me was, "How is your book doing?" I said it was doing very well until this virus caused a slowdown. I had signed a copy of my book and gave it to him. He was really glad to get it.

He said that his family had moved their oldest daughter out of her apartment at UAB last week because that university was going to close before the end of the school year to prevent the spread of the virus.

Our governor also closed all public schools before the end of the school year. So sad for many seniors of the class of 2020.

Since this was the last day we could go places before the shelter in place, Jay and I went to get gas in our car. Then we delivered a gift bag to our pastor's doorstep for Malachi, one of his sons, because it was his 4th birthday. Then we went to Menlo pharmacy to pick up a prescription and got a few groceries at Lucky's.

Our yard man, Preston, came at 3:00 p.m. to cut our grass. He told us that he was worried that he may not be allowed to mow yards during the next week due to the shelter-in-place order. God help him to be able to mow people's yards and earn income.

Our friend Savannah called and told us that her mom was having heart problems again. God help her and her mom.

In Tokyo, Amy said that Matthew and Quinn, his friend from school, had taken pictures of each other next to art walls in the city. She texted me a few of the pictures. So glad they are so creative. God, please watch over Amy, Dillon, Zach, and Matthew in Tokyo.

When we got home from Menlo, there were two packages on our doorstep. One was a photo book that I had put together for Matthew's 12th birthday from Shutterfly. The other package was from Mallika in Seattle. Lots of goodies! She had sent several kinds of cookies, nuts, and pancake mix. I texted her a thank you. Steven had let us know that he was coming back here tomorrow, so he would get to enjoy some of these snacks.

Mallika said that she was doing well and just wanted all this to be over. She said that she had made a list of things she wants to do when life gets back to normal. God bless her and keep her safe.

On Friday April 3, Steven texted and let us know he would be home at 6:00 p.m., after he does a trail run on the perimeter trail in Sewanee, Tennessee, on his way back.

There were no new positive CV cases in Tennessee or Chattooga County today. So we definitely had something to be grateful for.

For dinner, Jay and I got pizzas at Little Caesars. Steven got home about 15 minutes after we did. We had salads and pizza. Then cake and ice cream for dessert. We were so glad he made it home safely!

Saturday, April 4, 2020. Amy called us by FaceTime and showed us her forehead. She said that a cup from a shelf in her kitchen cupboard had fallen out and hit her when she opened the door. There was a red mark on her forehead and probably will heal in a couple of days. Thankfully no open wound.

She said that some of the restaurants in Tokyo were still open, but they weren't going out. The parks were closed now. Their family was only going out when they had to pick up groceries.

Amy told us that Zach and Matthew's school was closed for the end of the school year. They are still studying online to finish 8th grade and 6th grade. Their teachers are trying to prepare all the kids about not seeing their school friends again. It's especially hard for those who will be going back to the US in the summer. Amy said that they might not be able to say goodbye to their friends in person. Therefore, no closure.

This virus is taking a toll on relationships too. Dear God, make a way for Amy, Dillon, Zach, and Matthew to see some of their friends before they leave for the USA.

CHAPTER 27

Good News, an Easter Storm, and Steven Goes Back to Oregon

On Wednesday, April 8, 2020, I woke up at 2:30 a.m. but went back to sleep. Around 5:00 a.m., I woke up again and remembered that I had received some of Amy's mail; it was forwarded to us from Charlotte. I needed to take pictures of the mail and send them to her. It was around 6:00 p.m. in Tokyo, so I texted her the pictures. I told her to have a good evening. I was expecting her to say, "Thank you and have a good day."

Instead, she texted back, "Thank you. And we just learned that we may be coming back to the US sooner than expected. Have you been praying, Mom?"

What?

How wonderful! I told her we'd all been praying for this. "I can visualize you and Dillon and Zach and Matthew standing in your house in Charlotte and being really happy."

Amy said that the EY mobility consultants had contacted

them. They said their family should leave Japan as soon as possible in order to get a flight out. The consultants were coming tomorrow to evaluate their furniture for the move.

That sounded great to me. We should know more about their new plans later in the week. Now we just have to pray that the restrictions due to the virus are lessened so that we can go to North Carolina to see them.

Today's CV numbers in North Carolina were only thirty-four positives. In Georgia, there were 334 positives today.

Dear Lord, please remove this virus from our cities, states, and all countries around the world. Amen.

On Friday, April 10, 2020, Amy sent us a picture of Chubbs. She said that Matthew had taken it, and we thought it was so good.

Jay and I took a walk on our street and saw some beautiful purple flowers. Several of our neighbors have been taking walks most every day too. We waved at our neighbors. It's a great day with temps about 60 degrees, and it was sunny.

Steven texted. He just had to complete the trim on the window he installed at his house in Nashville. Then he's going to run at Percy Warner Park before he comes back to Georgia tomorrow.

Saturday, April 11, 2020, had no new positive CV cases in Tennessee. Steven is on his way home from Nashville. He installed the new window in one day by himself, using our ladder, which he had borrowed. All he has left to do is paint it next week.

He brought bagels from Panera Bread in Nashville for our lunch. Jay had an everything bagel, I had a plain bagel, and Steven had a blueberry bagel and part of a cinnamon bagel. I had been craving a Panera bagel, and it tasted great!

Jay cooked hot dogs on our grill for dinner. I fixed a salad and made a cake. It was so good to be together.

Amy called and wished us, "Happy Easter" since it was Sunday morning in Tokyo. She said that her family has a small balcony outside their bedroom in their apartment on the fifth floor of their building. They had not used it much before the quarantine, but now they're sitting outside and eating some of their meals while pretending they're eating at their favorite restaurants.

She said their plans to come home had stalled because they could not ship Chubbs yet. Maybe the kitty will have to come back on the plane with them.

Dear Lord, please work out this issue with the airlines. Let their kitty be able to come home with them.

As we were talking with Amy, Steven got a call from Mallika. I placed my phone in front of Steven's phone so that Amy and Mallika could talk to each other. It was so cool!

After the calls, Steven, Jay, and I took a walk down our street. We always enjoy doing that.

Sunday, April 12, 2020, was Easter Sunday. We watched Franklin Graham's televised service from a field hospital set up by Samaritan's Purse in New York City. He had a Michael W. Smith as his guest musician, which was so nice. Rev. Graham spoke about impossible circumstances in the Bible where Jesus performed miracles, such as a man blind from birth and a leper who asked Jesus to heal him. He talked about how no one knows how to cure this virus, but we all need to turn to Jesus and ask Him to come into our lives. It was inspiring.

For lunch I prepared meat loaf, green beans, macaroni and cheese, potato salad, and rolls. It tasted so good. Around 7:30 p.m., we were eating cake and ice cream when our phones alarmed with the news that we should take cover due to a tornado warning in our area. All three of us got our jackets, hats, and flashlights and went down into our basement. We heard the tornado sirens going off from downtown. We stayed in the basement for about an hour, until we heard the rain slowing down. Then we walked up the back stairs and saw that our power was on. We went to sleep after that.

In the morning, we found out there were eight tornadoes in our area last night. I saw pictures of the town of Trion on my phone, and it looked like the flash floods of 1990, when the river flooded into the high school. The school was relocated up the hill in 1995, so that wasn't a problem now.

Thank You, Lord, for keeping us safe.

On Thursday, April 16, 2020, there were no new CV cases in Oregon. Steven is making his way back there next week. Today he is in Nashville, painting the trim on his new window and cutting his grass, hopefully for the last time at his house. The report on his appraisal should be available tomorrow. If the new homeowner approves the updates, closing will be April 23.

Dear Lord, let everything be approved for this to happen.

It's been a wonderful few weeks having Steven here with us. But it's time for him to go back to the West Coast as Mallika misses him, and his A-frame house needs some

TLC. While he has been here, he has helped us so much. He cleaned out our gutters, changed multiple light bulbs, fixed our pipes under the sink, and cut down a huge limb over our driveway. He brought a humidifier from Nashville for us to use in our basement too. God bless him all his life.

On Saturday, April 18, I fixed some huckleberry pancakes from the mix Mallika sent us in her care package from Washington. After that, Steven and I took a walk and talked about his house. He should hear about the appraisal soon.

I posted on FB about Steven leaving from Atlanta today. My sister, Leigh Anne, saw this and texted that Jay and I should come by their house on our way back from the airport. I said we could be there at 1:30 p.m. We took Steven to the Atlanta airport. He told us that he would see us soon, and he loved us. Godspeed, Steven!

He had a good flight to Las Vegas but had a three-hour layover before his flight to Seattle. During that layover, he got a call from his real estate agent in Nashville with good news. The appraisal on his house was good.

We had a nice visit with Leigh Anne and Stanley in Atlanta and then drove home.

Steven made it to Seattle about 1:30 a.m. our time. Mallika picked him up at the airport. I'm so glad he's there safely.

CHAPTER 28

Matthew's Twelfth Birthday and Plans to Come Home

Matthew turned twelve on Tuesday, April 21, 2020. Amy FaceTimed us yesterday at 6:50 p.m. (7:50 a.m. in Tokyo) so we could sing "Happy Birthday" to him. She brought the cards and gifts we had sent him so that he could open them on his birthday. Matthew was still sleepy, but he woke up enough to open his card from us and read it aloud. Then he opened the photo book that I had made for him and read the front page. It included pictures of him from every year of his life. I hope this will be meaningful to him. Amy told us that she and Dillon gave him some extra cash because they won't be able to have a birthday party due to the quarantine.

I prayed, "Dear Lord, let their family be able to come back to the United States soon. And let Zach and Matthew be able to have birthday parties next year."

Our governor, Brian Kemp, announced today that they were allowing some businesses, such as hair salons and bowling alleys, to reopen for business this coming Friday. On

Monday, restaurants can open if they use social distancing and other guidelines. There has been such a backlash of mean comments in the news and on other media. People just need to be kind and use common sense, like wearing masks in stores and being aware of distance in groups.

Our church's secretary told us her sister is a hairdresser and is making masks for her clients. She said her sister has been receiving lots of calls since many people haven't been able to get a haircut in several weeks. She plans to have one customer at a time in her shop, and have other clients stay in their cars until she is ready for them.

Concerning our church services, our pastor and other local pastors had a conference call with Governor Kemp on Tuesday. It was decided to continue our virtual church services on Facebook for now. That is a wise choice since a large percentage of our members are senior citizens.

Dear Lord, please protect our family and friends. Remove this virus from our cities, states, and countries.

Thursday, April 23, is the closing date on Steven's Nashville house. It's been several months since he put it up for sale. Steven went back to Oregon a couple of weeks ago, and we haven't heard from him for a while.

Jay and I took our morning walk and then went for a drive. Morning walks are one of the highlights of our improved health regimens brought on by this pandemic.

In the afternoon, Steven called us on FaceTime and told us the sale went through for his house. He was really happy with the virtual process. The person buying the house had a walk-through with his real estate agent and was happy with all the improvements Steven completed while he was there. So all went well.

Steven's girlfriend, Mallika, was in the background on the FaceTime, working in the kitchen of Steven's cabin in La Pine. She waved and smiled. Steven said she had been cooking and preparing extra so they could freeze the food for Steven to have later. They were going to go on a hike soon and take some things to the local recycling center. When the returned, they were going to cook hamburgers to celebrate. We told him congratulations.

Now he plans to add a full bathroom to his A-frame and a stairway to his loft. God, thank You for blessing Steven with this sale and with Mallika.

At the end of the call, we told Steven we missed him and thanked him again for helping us while he was here in March and April. He told us that he liked fixing things, and it was fun. And he missed us too.

We said, "We love you. Bye for now." Is there anything better than to hear those words from your child?

Thank You, God, for blessing us with the best children and grandchildren ever!

A few days later, Sunday, April 26, we got a call from Amy. They had plane tickets to come back to the United States June 11! She hoped they could come home earlier, but Dillon needed to complete his work from home on Japan time. Zach and Matthew are finishing up their school years virtually too. Zach is graduating from middle school. The school is planning a ceremony in which each student goes to the school separately and films their individual parts of the graduation at ASIJ. Amy said that she was outvoted about returning earlier 3 to 1. But it's only six more weeks, and there was a lot of planning and packing to do. And Chubbs will be able to ride on the same airplane with them.

Amy showed us Matthew and Zach in their rooms. Then Chubbs was with her in the living room. Everyone seemed happy. Prayers for the time to pass quickly for their return.

Jay and I watched a Hallmark movie, one of the episodes of *"Signed, Sealed, Delivered.* Here's a quote we heard: "There are no small miracles; they're all big. They might look small because we stand back from them."

On Tuesday, April 28, 2020, I texted Amy a picture that I had taken of a bill that was forwarded from their house in Charlotte. This had been our routine for three years; her US mail was forwarded to our address in Georgia. I would take a picture of the mail and send it to her. She could pay it electronically or mail it. She responded with, "Thank you, Mom." Then she mentioned that she and Dillon were going outside for a walk since it was a beautiful day in Tokyo. I told her that Jay and I were taking walks in our neighborhood every day now. Only a few short weeks, and she and her family will be back in Charlotte.

In current Georgia news, by midnight April 30, the shelter-in-place order for everyone under sixty-five will be lifted. But social distancing may continue for months or years. Nearly every store has tape on the floor or signs that mark six feet apart. We're still wearing masks in public places.

Dear Lord, help us begin to return to being able to go places and see our friends and family. Let us not forget to return to You.

On Saturday, we went to Ingles for our weekly groceries and wore our masks. Since we hadn't been there in weeks, I thought that no one would recognize us. I was wrong. As soon as we walked in the front door, one of the managers said hello and that she was glad to see us. I thought, *Oh, I guess we're not incognito.* I cleaned the handle of our cart with a sanitizer wipe and went toward the produce aisle. As soon as we got to the fruit, one of the produce employees, Josh (also a friend from church), looked at us and said, "Your glasses are fogging up." I thought that I was rocking the safety look, but I was "shot down" in the first aisle. Ha!

We talked about how our lives were going, mostly just going to get groceries once a week and then home. Josh said he goes to work each day and then goes home. We said to tell his family hello, which he said he would. It was so good to see him. We finished our grocery shopping and went home. Our secretive shopping trip was not so secret.

It was now May 2, and we decided to take some grocery care packages to some of the families who go to our church and have been helping with the virtual services that are online each Sunday. Stephen Peppers and his brother, Stanton, recorded the services and posted them on Facebook Live. Their dad, Barry, preached several of those messages when our pastor, Sean, was in quarantine. Don and Teresa sang hymns and played music for them.

The Peppers family sent us a creative thank-you note in which each family member wrote a personal sentence. The youngest son, Stetson, who is also in my Sunday school class, drew a picture of his family. We will be so glad when we can see them again.

When we took a bag to Don and Teresa's house, we stood beside our car and talked to Don for several minutes. Jay told him that he had been practicing "I Need Thee Every Hour" on the piano. Don said that it would be nice if Jay played the song when they recorded the FB service on Thursday. Jay and I went to our church then, and it was so good to see Don and Teresa, Pastor Sean, and Stephen. Only six people were there, but it felt like we were finally with people again, though we were distanced throughout the sanctuary.

Sean preached a message on Philippians chapter 1, talked about how the apostle Paul had to go through many trials, and how he wrote letters to the churches who supported him. Paul often used military terms. In verses 27–30, the term, "striving together," was like being side by side in a wall of shields where soldiers support each other.

Sean also said we could all throw away our 2020 planners since we have had to change our plans so many times.

Long before we existed, God knew 2020 was going to be one of the most challenging in history. We need to learn a lesson from this before it's ever completely better.

Sean has had double pneumonia this past month. This was his first sermon in which he was able to stand the whole time he talked. After he was finished, he said he needed a nap.

Prayers for Sean to feel better soon. Prayers also for Danielle, his wife, who is expecting their fourth son in a few weeks. God doesn't just give four sons to anyone. It's a lot of responsibility. God help their family. Keep them safe and well!

In our family news, Steven called Friday evening and said he is having a contractor draw up plans for an addition that includes a bathroom and laundry for his A-frame. He told me Mallika is in the final process of being approved for her new position in Portland. She has gone through many virtual interviews and one live interview at a coffee shop; they couldn't have it at the hospital due to restrictions. Her new job will begin in the fall. That's so exciting because she will be only four hours from Steven instead of eight hours away in Seattle.

We're expecting a phone call from Amy this evening. We'll discuss our plans to see them in June. When she called on FaceTime, she was sitting on their couch in the living room next to a picture window. It looked like a beautiful sunny day. Dillon said hello to us. Then Matthew came in the room too. He's growing up fast. She showed us their kitty, who was at their feet on the carpet. Amy said Chubbs was flying back to the United States with them in June. Dillon will have the cat carrier under his seat. That should be interesting. At least they will all be coming back to the United States together.

Amy also said some of their neighbors and friends in Charlotte are going to clean and stain their deck at their house so they can use it.

We talked about coming to see them in June in Charlotte, a few days after they get back. She told us they're renting furniture for the whole house until their furniture arrives from Tokyo, which takes several months. They will have a queen guest bed in Charlotte. All we need to bring are our luggage and ourselves. We are so looking forward to it!

Only a few more weeks until we see them again!

CHAPTER 29

Lights Out Can Be a Good Thing and Zach's Graduation

Zach in soccer uniform.

Around 2:20 a.m. May 5, 2020, our power went out due to a thunderstorm. During the early morning hours, I had gotten up to get a drink of water and saw the light in my closet going dim. Then it totally went out. I felt my way back to my bed and looked at my phone.

I heard my phone ding since I had the ringer on. It was about 3:30 p.m. in Tokyo, and Amy had texted me a great picture of Zach. He was dressed in a light-blue checked shirt and black pants. He was holding a red soccer ball, which he was going to use in his graduation picture to represent his membership on the middle school soccer team. Amy told me the ASIJ was having a virtual graduation ceremony on June 9, only two days before they fly home to Charlotte. She said she would send me the graduation details soon. I texted her back and told her that Zach looked so handsome.

Then she texted, "Oh, I'm so sorry to wake you up!" She just realized that it was only 2:30 a.m. in Georgia. I told her I was awake because our power had gone out due to a storm, so it was fine.

I then called NGEMC to report the outage electronically. When I was on the fourth phase of answering the questions on my keypad, our power came back on. I texted Amy, "Our power is back on, and thank you for praying."

"That was fast," she replied. "I hope you can get back to sleep soon." I slept like a baby for two more hours. It's great to have a daughter who prays for you in the middle of the night.

Love and prayers for Amy, Dillon, Zach, and Matthew. Can't wait to see you all soon.

My Wednesday, May 6, 2020, started with me texting Amy information about some of her routine mail to Tokyo.

It was evening in Japan, and Amy told me they had a storm with thunder and lightning, which is unusual for Tokyo.

Thursday, May 7, began with the news that other states besides Georgia are opening some of their businesses. Georgia has had a 14 percent increase in employment since reopening April 23. That's a very good sign!

Our church, First Baptist, is set to have a limited reopening on Sunday, May 17 for those who can come and feel safe with social distancing, and so on. Pastor Sean said that no one will be policing the congregation for anyone who might forget and accidentally shake someone's hand. And no one will tackle you if you hug someone. I think we're all used to virtual hugs by now, even though we don't have to like it. At least it's a step toward normalcy and moving toward a "new normal" worship experience.

God watch over us and help us.

That evening we filmed our Mother's Day service to be shown on Sunday, May 10. Don and Teresa sang a medley of hymns, including "Savior Like a Shepherd Lead Us," "Open My Eyes, Lord," and, "Lord, Prepare Me to Be a Sanctuary." All so very appropriate for the times we're in. Then they sang "Surely Goodness and Mercy." Psalm 23 is my favorite psalm, and those verses speak to daily life during this pandemic.

We need to trust, pray, and believe that God is beside us.

Jay sang "Give Me Jesus." We had first seen this song performed by Fernando Ortega for the memorial service of Rev. Billy Graham's wife, Ruth. Jay had sung this song for the funerals of a few of our church members in the past few years.

While he was singing it tonight, Amy sent me a picture

of Matthew and Chubbs. It's always so good to hear from them. They're so anxious to be back in the United States. Then we will be in the same time zone. God help everything to go well for their move home.

The next day, Jay and I went to the local grocery store to get our groceries for the week. While we were in the parking lot, putting the groceries in our car, we heard someone say, "There are my friends from First Baptist."

We turned around and I, "Are you Bishop Hardin?"

"Yes, I am. And I remember that I saw you and your son at the Atlanta airport at Christmastime. You told me about your book about your son and his races."

I told him I had been wanting to give him a signed copy of that I had a book in the car, so I signed it and gave it to him.

Bishop Hardin said that he wants to tell his congregation about my book. Then he said, "You all, please never change."

I replied, "We don't plan to change."

That was a divine appointment for sure.

Saturday evening, Amy called to wish me a happy Mother's Day. She told me that Dillon made chocolate chip pancakes with strawberries for her breakfast. He was now cleaning the kitchen. She called for Zach and Matthew to sit next to her, and they told me, "Happy Mother's Day," too. Amy showed me Chubbs, who was near their feet on a rug. And she told me she'd ordered the rental furniture for their home in Charlotte.

I asked her how she was feeling, and she said that the heating pad helps. On Tuesday, she texted that she was feeling miraculously better and had a doctor's appointment just to be sure everything was okay.

I had forwarded some pictures of her mail to her. She commented that soon the dates on the mail would be after their return to the States. I told her, "That's good news all around."

Amy told us their favorite Tokyo restaurant was taking to-go orders. That's unusual for restaurants in Tokyo, but she was so glad to have that option. They will be able to enjoy some of their favorite Mexican food while they are still in Japan.

Amy, Dillon, Zach, and Matthew have self-quarantined in their apartment since February. This week Amy is allowing Zach to meet his school friend Axel at a local park, so they can play soccer. Zach has to ride his dad's bicycle since he's grown so tall. His bicycle from two years ago is now too small for him.

Matthew met his friend Quinn to take pictures of each other near an art wall with painted wings on it. Matthew told me that Quinn and his parents moved back to their vacation home in Colorado. Matthew had tears in his eyes when he told me, so it must have been a sudden decision. He didn't get to say goodbye to Quinn in person, just on FaceTime. I hope they will get to see each other again.

Zach graduates from middle school in a virtual ceremony in June. He won't get to say goodbye to most of his friends either. Each student will go to the school at an assigned time and have their part of the graduation recorded. The year 2020 has been difficult for him too. God, watch over Zach and help him each day.

Preparations are continuing in Charlotte for Amy their return. Amy told us that their neighbor Jeff painted most of the rooms in their house. He also retiled the floor in their laundry room. All this, and he renovated his own master bath too. He and Emily, his wife, and their daughters, Abby and Kate, have been such good friends over the years. They seem very happy that Amy's family is returning soon. Along with their good friends Kristen and Brad and their sons, Jake and Jack, who have been wonderful to help out so much. Brad and Jeff got together to stain Amy and Dillon's back deck so that they can use it for cookouts when they return.

It's so great to have friends like them. Thank You, God, for their friends!

CHAPTER 30

Mid-May: Books and Losing a Brother-in-Law

Wednesday, May 14, was cool and rainy. We were on our way to pick up some food for lunch and two of our friends, Charlie and Ruth, had asked me for a copy of my book, *Steven: A Runner's Life*. Their house was on the way, so I called Ruth and told her I would leave a copy in a shopping bag on their door. I also included some small bags of peanuts for snacks. Charlie and Ruth are both in their nineties and had been quarantined for months. As I was backing the car out of their driveway after dropping off the bag, Ruth came out of the house and waved. She said it would be so good to be able to come back to church when this is over. I waved and said, "That's so true." Charlie later texted me to thank me for the book and the peanuts. They said they would enjoy reading it! Ruth is a retired English teacher, so I'm sure she loves to read. They are a precious couple. God bless them.

In this Coronavirus-19 era, we've been excited to hear new sounds while taking our walks in our neighborhood.

Like a jet overhead or a train whistle near downtown. About a month ago, the sounds were few and far between. There are now more sounds as people venture outside more.

On Saturday, May 16, the first sounds we heard as we walked was a large cow going, "Moo." It reminded me of the cow in Steven's 2015 YouTube video from his 100-mile race in Idaho called the Bear 100-Epic Weather. He came upon a cow near the trail who doesn't want any runners crossing its path, so the cow mooed very loudly. When we heard the cow in our neighborhood, we determined that it had to be in a fenced-in a yard behind our street. It was just so funny to hear it.

Amy called us that evening to tell me Tokyo had fewer than a hundred positive test reports, and it was decreasing. People there were allowed to be outside in the parks, and the weather was in the sixties and sunny. That is good news.

I told her that our church in Summerville was starting services tomorrow with social distancing. It will be so good to see our friends in person! Dear Lord, thank You for keeping all of us safe and healthy for the last seventy days. And protect us in the days ahead.

Sunday morning, Jay's sister, Kitty, called him and said Tommy, his brother-in-law, was admitted to a local hospital with a low sodium level and possible heart issues. We told her we would pray for him.

The next Sunday morning, May 24, Jay and I had the feeling that we should get in touch with Kitty. Jay texted her, and we waited for a reply.

For the next two hours, we ate breakfast and got ready to go to church. Then around 10:00 a.m., Kitty called us and told us that Tommy had just passed away. Then she told us what happened.

On Saturday, Tommy had been in the hospital in Rome and asked Kitty if he could go home. She asked the nurse if that was possible. The nurse said she would send a hospice nurse to talk to them. After talking with her, they made preparations for a hospital bed to be sent to their home. Then Kitty and Tommy went home. His mother, Doris, stayed with them overnight. About five o'clock on Sunday morning, Tommy woke up and talked to his mom and Kitty. Then he slipped into a coma and passed away before the hospice nurse could get there.

We decided to go to Kitty's house. On the way, we stopped at a grocery store to get some ham, cheeses, sub rolls, chips, and a cheesecake for them to have food for lunch. We talked to Kitty and Doris for a good while before Kitty said she was getting hungry and was going to fix a sandwich, and did we want to eat too? We all had some fresh sandwiches that were so good.

Kitty said more friends and family had let them know they were on the way to the house. Jay and I hugged her and said that we would go home and come back to see her soon.

By Wednesday, Kitty and Doris had made the arrangements for Tommy's service on Monday of the next week. The chapel service was scheduled for 11:00 a.m. It was for immediate family only due to COVID-19 restrictions. Kitty asked Jay to play several hymns. Jay said he would play several hymns before the service and then "Amazing Grace," Tommy's favorite, at the beginning of the service.

Rev. Billy Fricks, a friend of the family, gave the eulogy. He talked about how God selected craftsmen to build the pillars of the temple in the Old Testament. Then workmen were assigned to frame the temple of Solomon. He said that Tommy was proud of the construction work he did his whole life. He likened it to a biblical workman who was not ashamed. Rev. Billy also read Psalm 23. After the prayer, Jay played "How Great Thou Art." All of Tommy's children and most of his grandchildren were there.

After the chapel service, we drove in the procession to Oak Knoll Cemetery, near the Rome Cinemas in West Rome. It rained steadily the whole way. About six patrol cars from the Rome Police Force accompanied us there. When we pulled into the cemetery, we saw about fifty people there. Everyone had umbrellas.

Jay and I parked and then went to the graveside. We stood outside the covered area. After the service, we saw our close family, our nephew, Robby, and Natalie, his wife, along with their oldest daughter, Adair. Natalie said they were social distancing. I said we were too. But I hugged them anyway since I hadn't seen them for months, and none of us have shown any symptoms. We invited them to come to Kitty's house afterwards. They came, and we had a good visit. I gave Adair a signed copy of my book. One of Kitty's good friends also asked for a copy. My unwritten rule is that if anyone asks me for a copy of my book, I will give them one. Some people pay for it, but for some, I just give them a copy.

> It will come back eventually. You can't out give God. (Malachi 3:10)

CHAPTER 31

An Anniversary, an Eighth Grade Graduation, and Future School Plans

On evening of Saturday, May 30, 2020, Amy called us from Japan; it was Sunday morning there. She told us she was going for a walk with a friend in Tokyo. Dillon had left at 6:30 that morning to go golfing with some work friends. Several of his friends had gone in together to give Dillon an Amazon gift card since he was leaving for the United States in two weeks. Amy said he would be gone all day.

Zach was still asleep, and Matthew was online with his friend Quinn, who was now in Colorado. Amy said that she, Zach, and Matthew had been invited to a friend's house for lunch. The friend is the mother of Zach's good friend, Axel, who is in Zach's class at ASIJ. Axel's family is from Sweden. They had a really nice time.

Amy also told us Zach was entered in the lottery for CATA—Central Academy of Technology and Arts—in Monroe, North Carolina, a charter school. She forwarded all Zach's grades and test scores, and the school accepted them. The lottery would be drawn the last week in June.

Dear Lord, let Zach go to the school You have prepared for him. In Jesus's name, Amen.

On Monday, June 1, at 8:00 p.m., I texted pictures of some of Amy's mail that had come to us. I realized that it was 9:00 a.m. on June 2 in Tokyo. So I said, "Happy anniversary."

Amy and Dillon got married on June 2, 2001, at the Cliffs at Glassy in Landrum, South Carolina. Dillon had seen the chapel when he played golf there. Dave, his roommate at the time, had been working there as a security guard and told Dillon how beautiful it was. I sent Amy a picture I took on her wedding day.

Amy said the picture brought to mind sweet memories. To celebrate their anniversary, the whole family was going out to a restaurant to eat yakinika, steak cooked over an open flame. I believe it will be the first time that they will have eaten out as a family in three months. I know it was great!

Praying for many more happy years!

Jay and I planned to cook hamburgers and hot dogs on the grill Saturday, June 6. After I made a breakfast of bacon, scrambled eggs, and toast, we took a walk down our street. When we came home, Jay got out our Weber grill so we could cook out around lunch time. I made up the hamburger patties and put them on a plate to go into the refrigerator until it was time to cook them. Jay got the charcoal started after he moved the grill into the shade under a tree at the end of our driveway. We put some lawn chairs near the tree and sat and enjoyed the weather. Jay said that a few of our neighbors drove by and waved. I brought the hamburgers out to grill and saw Ted and Marilyn drive by on their golf cart. During this time of staying at home, our street was ideal for people to ride on in their golf carts and ATVs. And we've enjoyed walking several times a day.

Amy FaceTimed us Saturday evening. This would be the last time she would call us from their Tokyo apartment. She said the movers were coming in an hour to start packing. It's supposed to take them about four days. Amy showed us her kitchen, where she had packed all the suitcases that were going with them to the hotel. She had labeled items in the kitchen for the movers. Zach was sitting on the couch in their living room and told us hi. Then Matthew came from his bedroom and waved at us.

I told Amy I had been looking at my journal that morning and saw where she told me about Matthew's first day of school in Japan, which would have been fourth grade. He told her that one of the boys in his class had asked him, "Do you want to be friends?"

When Matthew answered yes, they played and talked on the playground. When he got home, Amy asked him what his friend's name was, and Matthew said, "I don't know. I forgot to ask him." The next day at school, Matthew found out that his friend's name was Keita. They would be friends the whole time they lived in Japan. God has blessed their whole family with good friends.

On Monday, June 8, Amy sent me a link to Zach's eighth-grade promotion/graduation ceremony from the ASIJ. It would be a virtual ceremony on YouTube beginning at 5:00 a.m. EDT. We were excited to be able to see pictures of Zach and his friends who were also graduating.

They were moving to a local hotel for the next few days. The movers would be packing their dishes and furniture to go in a metal shipping container to be shipped back to North Carolina. Amy said they had to turn in the phones they used in Japan before they got on the plane. Dillon's North Carolina phone would be the only one available until they could get new phones in the United States. It turns out that she was able to send messages through her laptop computer when she had Wi-Fi available in between flights.

At 4:45 Tuesday morning, I went into our living room and enabled the link to YouTube that Amy sent us for Zach's ceremony at ASIJ. Jay and I were both able to see the pictures of Zach's school. There were photos of the school with the Japanese flag and the US flag and beautiful music playing. At 5:00 a.m. EDT, 6:00 p.m. JST, the announcer began introducing the principal, vice principal, and three student speakers chosen by their teachers from the eighth-grade class. All the speeches were very encouraging. One of the students, Zayne, talked about how he was so shy in sixth grade that he felt invisible. But then he started speaking up in school situations. He said it became easier to find his voice after that.

They showed videos of each of the more than one hundred, which was interesting. Then they showed the homerooms with groups of ten students with each of their teachers. They were taken at the beginning of the school year.

Zach's personal video was taken in their apartment. He was wearing a nice, blue, dress shirt and dark pants. The video showed him walking across their living room in front of the large picture window.

Some of the music they played was familiar, including Pachelbel's "Canon" because Jay played that song for several weddings. Also a Coldplay tune called "Viva La Vida," which means, "Long Live Life."

We really enjoyed the ceremony and were so impressed with all the coordination and time it took to put it together.

Best of luck to Zach and all the graduates until they meet again.

CHAPTER 32

Coming Home

On Thursday, June 11, 2020, Amy, Dillon, Zach, Matthew, and Chubbs left Tokyo for the United States at 4:45 p.m. JST (3:45 a.m. EDT). I had been awake since 1:30 a.m. I thought that I would only be able to get updates on my flight tracker app. But through God's providence, when they landed in Seattle nine hours later, Amy found Wi-Fi access and let us know they were okay. That was such a relief. And as Amy said, "We're back in the US for good."

They changed planes to go to Detroit and then once again to go to Charlotte. Around 1:30 a.m. EDT, Amy sent me a message that they had gotten to their home in Charlotte, taken showers, and were settling in for the night. Praise the Lord!

The next morning, while Jay and I were walking on our street after breakfast, my phone lit up. Amy calling us on FaceTime. She looked so happy that she was glowing. "I just thought I would call you in real time." She had gotten up at 8:00 a.m. and everyone else got up at 8:30. She said it was great to be able to walk outside just by opening the front door. From their apartment in Tokyo, they had to walk down a hallway, go down five flights of stairs or take an elevator, and then pass a concierge to go outside.

This was much better, and it was a beautiful day in Charlotte. She took us on a virtual tour of their house. She went upstairs to Zach's room, where four teenage boys—Zach, Matthew, Jack, and Jake—were sitting and talking.

Then she went downstairs and told us Chubbs had done so well on the flight. When they got to their house, the kitty remembered it and went into every room. They had to put a bell on her collar for traveling, and she still had it on. They could hear the jingle of her bell wherever she went in the house.

We told Amy we would be driving to Charlotte on Monday afternoon, like we had already arranged. She said they would be happy to see us whatever time we got there.

Jay and I are so happy they're home safely. It will be great to see them on Monday!

God is so good!

Jay and I traveled to Charlotte on the morning of June 15. I texted Amy on Messenger and hoped she would be able to see it since they hadn't gotten their new phones yet. But in just a few minutes, Amy messaged me back that they were really glad we were on the way and to keep them posted on our progress. We stopped at the Cracker Barrel in Gaffney, South Carolina, for lunch. Then we went to the North Carolina Welcome Station, where we saw beautiful yellow day lilies.

When we got to Amy's house at 2:30 p.m., everyone was at the front door to greet us. It was great to be able to hug them after six months. Dillon, Zach, and Jay got our suitcases out of the car and took them upstairs to the guest room. Chubbs greeted us too. She remembered us and let us pet her, even though it had been two and a half years since we saw her last.

Over the next few days, Amy had several of her friends over to visit. We saw their neighbor Jeff, who is a high school principal. He had done so much to help them with their house, like painting several rooms and setting up their televisions. And he installed a new ceiling fan in their family room on Friday while we were there. We also saw Zach's former soccer coach, Brad and his son, Aidan, who is a longtime friend and teammate. Brad earned his PhD degree from Duke this year. We also saw his wife, Jenny, and Grace, their daughter. It's always a blessing to be around them.

While we were visiting, Amy's friend Kristen came over, and we got to talk. She told us she really enjoyed visiting our nice house in Summerville, Georgia, a year ago, when she came for Jay's seventieth birthday party. I was pleasantly surprised and happy that she had a good time. She said it was so relaxing being around us and sitting in the living room with all our family. Kristen told me she looked around and saw Amy's awards from high school and college in her room. Then she also saw Steven's awards in his room. She couldn't believe all they have achieved since they came from the small town of Summerville. I told her it was all due to prayer, many prayers said over them every day of their lives.

Speaking of prayer, Kristen asked me to pray for Monday, June 22, the day names are drawn in the CATA student lottery to admit students to the ninth grade. Her son Jack and our grandson Zach are in that drawing. I assured her, "Of course, I will pray for them."

On Monday, June 22, Amy messaged me with the results of the lottery. Jack, Ben, and Jason, three of Zach's friends, were selected. Zach was on the waiting list and could be chosen in the next few days. I know it's difficult to have to wait, but sometimes God has plans we don't understand.

Over the next two days, we all prayed and waited. Then on Wednesday, June 24, Amy texted that Zach had been accepted and was going to CATA. Yay! Zach also found out that the following Monday, June 29, he would begin soccer practice for high school soccer. Jack would be going to the practices too. That was exciting news all around!

It turned out that the soccer practices were in the morning, from 9:30 to 11:00, which gives them a break from the afternoon heat. Zach says he likes it.

Jay and I plan to come to some of the games in the fall to see Zach play. He's a very good player!

During the summer of 2020, we were able to have several good visits when Amy and her family came to see us. Once was in Georgia, when we drove to Cloudland. Then we took a road to the right, where we saw people hang gliding off a mountain. We also got to take a family vacation to South Carolina. Steven and Mallika came from Oregon to go with us to the Litchfield Beach Resort. We met Amy and her family there. We all had a great time going to the beach every day. In the evenings, we went to eat at some of our favorite places, like Quigleys, a local seafood restaurant. Kristen and her oldest son, Jake, came to eat with us for our forty-eighth anniversary at a new Japanese steak house called Hachiya. Jake is a eighteen months older than his brother, Jack, who is Zach's best friend. Jake is a very gifted basketball player and will probably have many offers to play at the college level. Can't wait to see what God has in store for him.

In November 2020, Dillon, Amy, Zach, and Matthew were going to the Cliffs in South Carolina to spend a few days. They invited us to come stay with them too. It was great fall weather, and we enjoyed many fun walks and watching movies with them in the evenings. We stayed at a lovely house near the picturesque thirteenth hole of the famous golf course there. We could see the lights of the city of Greenville at night from the top of the mountain. On our way home, we saw the sign for the Furman Golf Course, which brought back many good memories of our college days there, where Jay and I met fifty years ago.

CHAPTER 33

Epilogue: 2021— One Year Later

Amy and Dillon's twentieth wedding anniversary on June 2, 2021. They planned a full celebration with family and friends who had been in the wedding party and their children.

The week began with Amy and Dillon having some of their friends and Zach and Matthew's friends come to the Cliffs in South Carolina for golf, tennis, and swimming each day. Then Jay and I went to the Atlanta airport to pick up Steven and Mallika. They stayed at our house until Thursday, when we left for South Carolina. We met Amy, Dillon, Zach, and Matthew outside a restaurant at one of the golf clubs at the Cliffs. It was a beautiful sunny day, so we ate at a table on the porch there. Then we all drove to a nearby park and took a hike near the falls. Next we all went to the house where we would stay at the Cliffs. It was gorgeous. There was a sign on the door with an Irish blessing that said, "1,000 welcomes."

That evening we went to the Cliffs at Glassy clubhouse

for dinner. Unbeknown to Mallika, Steven planned to ask her to marry him at the chapel after dinner. The rest of us were in on the secret, so it was very exciting! We had a delicious dinner and then drove up the hill to the chapel. Since it was after 7:00, the sun was beginning to set. We took pictures of Amy and Dillon because this was the chapel where they were married twenty years ago.

Then Steven took Mallika's hand and said, "We're not just here to take pictures." He got down on one knee and said, "I love you and want to ask you to marry me." He had a ring in a beautiful wooden box engraved with her name and a mountain range on it. He opened the box and showed her.

"Yes. Yes, I'll marry you." Then she added, "That's the easiest yes that I've ever had to give." He put the ring on her finger, and they hugged. They turned to all of us as we clapped and cheered.

The first thing Mallika said to us was, "Did you know about this?"

I replied, "Yes, for at least two weeks. It was so hard not to give anything away." We all took turns hugging and celebrating this wonderful day as the sun was setting behind the mountains. It was glorious!

Amy and Dillon had a Friday lunch planned at the Cliffs clubhouse for their friends Matt and Laura, and their children, Madison and Ryan. Also their friends, Gene and Cindy and their children, Kate and Blake. Gene and Cindy actually met each other at Amy and Dillon's wedding and were married a few years later.

We all ate a wonderful lunch on the patio. At our table were Steven, Mallika, Jay, Zach, Matthew, and I. After the lunch, Mallika took photos of all the couples and friends.

Then the manager at the Cliffs took a picture of the whole group. Later, they had that picture printed and framed as an anniversary gift to Amy and Dillon.

In August was our annual family Litchfield Beach trip to South Carolina. Also in August, the delayed beginning of the Summer Olympics in Tokyo, which was postponed from 2020.

The Olympics began in July 2021. Since there was an increase in COVID-19 cases worldwide, the IOC decided to allow the Olympics to continue for the athletes, with daily testing and masks worn inside each venue. No family, friends, or local fans were allowed at the venues unless they were coaches or staff. NBC broadcast the competitions on their regular stations, USA network, CNBC, NBC Sports, and their streaming service, Peacock.

We watched many of the events. NBC commentators were so interesting and informative. But what made it extra special for us was the fact that Games were live from Tokyo, where Amy and her family lived from 2017 until 2020.

During the first week of the Olympics, Jay and I were in Summerville preparing for our trip to Pawley's Island. On Friday of that week, we drove to the Atlanta airport to pick up Steven. He was going to help us drive to the beach. His fiancée, Mallika, could not come this time because she was working.

Steven loves to watch the Olympics, especially the track and field events since he is an ultrarunner. In 1996, when the summer Olympics were held in Atlanta, Jay, Steven, and I were able to get tickets for a track and field event at Turner Field. We saw Jackie Joyner-Kersey in a preliminary race. Amy was in Madrid, Spain, for a summer semester between her junior and senior years at UGA or she would have been with us too.

On Monday morning, August 2, we left for South Carolina. We got to the registration area at the Litchfield by 4:00. Evidently many other people had the same idea because there were already about twenty people in line at the front desk. We parked our car and then got in line to wait. In less than an hour, we had our room keys and parking passes. Steven bought coffee for him and his dad at the Starbucks near the front desk. And he bought an iced strawberry lemonade for me. He also had time to call Mallika, who was on call at her hospital in Portland. She said that she is definitely planning on being with us at the beach next year.

Amy, Dillon, and the boys met us at our condo around 5:30 that evening. It was so good to see them and know that we would have several days together. They had stopped at the grocery store on the way. Dillon made us tacos for dinner that night. Then we all went to the beach, where the boys played football, and we took a walk at sunset. It was so fun. We even saw a young man on a skateboard that glowed on the sand. After we got back to our condo, we watched some of the Olympics.

It was raining too hard to go to the beach on Tuesday. We decided to go to the Sea Captains House for lunch in Myrtle Beach, about thirty minutes away. We had a wonderful meal. Then went to a movie called *Jungle Cruise*. That evening Dillon drove back to Charlotte, so he could complete his workweek. He told us that he plans to spend the whole week with us next year.

The rest of us spent Wednesday and Thursday going

from the beach to the pool to the lazy river. We had a wonderful, relaxing time. Wednesday evening, we ate dinner at a Japanese restaurant. We enjoyed watching the cook prepare our meal in front of us. He told Jay and I, "Happy anniversary," when he found out it was our forty-ninth. He invited us to come back next year, for our fiftieth. Yes, we plan to.

On Thursday, we went to Quigley's and had a great seafood dinner. When we returned to our condo, we watched more Olympic events, mostly swimming, beach volleyball, and track and field. There were so many inspiring stories about the athletes. And great commercials too.

What made it so much more interesting was that Amy and Dillon recognized many of the areas of Tokyo and Japan that were shown. They had shopped there and visited many of them when they lived there. Their main station/district was Shibuya, where Dillon caught a train to work at his building in Tokyo. It was also where they caught trains to go to other cities in Japan since they did not have a car while they lived there.

An interesting side story shown during the Olympics was about a store called the Cat Café, where people can pet and play with cats. Amy, Matthew, and Zach went there in 2017, before Chubbs joined them in Japan.

We learned that cats are considered good luck in Japan. It began as a legend about a cat born at the Gotoka-ji temple in Tokyo during the Edo period, 1603–1868. According to temple historians, the daimyo, or regional ruler, Il Naotoka, was saved from a lightning bolt when the abbot's pet cat, Tama, beckoned him into the temple while he was hunting with falcons.

The traditional waving cat is a popular figurine in Japan. It is named Maneki-neko in Japanese, which means, "beckoning cat." They have been bringing luck and prosperity for centuries and are popular in Chinatown and Asian stores around the world. The statue, with the right paw raised, attracts money and good fortune. A raised left paw invites friendship and customers. I've seen these in local nail salons as a welcome. Japan has so many interesting customs and traditions.

As we left Pawley's Island for another year, we also said goodbye to the 2020–2021 Summer Olympics. As always, we have hope for another year to come. And to the wedding of Steven and Mallika in March 2022. Jay and I are also looking forward to our fiftieth wedding anniversary on August 5, 2022, and our family beach trip to South Carolina.

Aurigato. Thank you in Japanese for all the great memories and those to come. We give our Lord thanks for every good thing in our lives! Thank You, Jesus!

God bless you, everyone!

Printed in the United States
by Baker & Taylor Publisher Services